MW01222106

WEST COAST MISSION

Bles...
our shared love
of Concordia!

Ron

see 1 '83

West Coast Mission

The Changing Nature
of Christianity in Vancouver

ROSS A. LOCKHART

McGill-Queen's University Press
Montreal & Kingston · London · Chicago

© McGill-Queen's University Press 2024

ISBN 978-0-2280-2285-5 (cloth)
ISBN 978-0-2280-2286-2 (paper)
ISBN 978-0-2280-2326-5 (ePDF)
ISBN 978-0-2280-2327-2 (ePUB)

Legal deposit fourth quarter 2024
Bibliothèque nationale du Québec

Printed in Canada on acid-free paper that is 100% ancient forest free
(100% post-consumer recycled), processed chlorine free

This book has been published with the help of a grant from the Federation for the
Humanities and Social Sciences, through the Awards to Scholarly Publications Program,
using funds provided by the Social Sciences and Humanities Research Council of Canada.

Financé par le gouvernement du Canada — Funded by the Government of Canada — Canada — Conseil des arts du Canada — Canada Council for the Arts

We acknowledge the support of the Canada Council for the Arts.

Nous remercions le Conseil des arts du Canada de son soutien.

McGill-Queen's University Press in Montreal is on land which long served as a site of
meeting and exchange amongst Indigenous Peoples, including the Haudenosaunee and
Anishinabeg nations. In Kingston it is situated on the territory of the Haudenosaunee
and Anishinaabek. We acknowledge and thank the diverse Indigenous Peoples whose
footsteps have marked these territories on which peoples of the world now gather.

Library and Archives Canada Cataloguing in Publication

Title: West Coast mission: the changing nature of Christianity in Vancouver /
Ross A. Lockhart.

Name: Lockhart, Ross A., author.

Description: Includes bibliographical references and index.

Identifiers: Canadiana (print) 20240368355 | Canadiana (ebook) 2024036838X |
ISBN 9780228022855 (cloth) | ISBN 9780228022862 (paper) |
ISBN 9780228023265 (ePDF) | ISBN 9780228023272 (ePUB)

Subjects: LCSH: Christianity—British Columbia—Vancouver. | LCSH: Christians—British
Columbia—Vancouver. | LCSH: Vancouver (B.C.)—Church history—21st century.

Classification: LCC BR580.V36 L63 2024 | DDC 277.11/33—dc23

This book was typeset by Marquis Interscript in 10.5/13 Sabon.
Copyediting by Eleanor Gasparik.

For Laura, Emily, Jack, and Sadie

Contents

Figures and Table

FIGURES

*Unless otherwise specified, all photos are courtesy of the author.

TABLE

Acknowledgments

Over several years of research, that included navigating the impact of a global pandemic, this ethnographic study of Christianity in Vancouver led me into fascinating conversations with diverse constituencies that proved to be a rich and rewarding process of discovery. I am grateful to all those who participated in coffee conversations, focus groups, and academic forums that helped shape my thinking and deepen my understanding of Christian expressions in Canada's largest West Coast city.

This book grows out of my PhD work at Vrije Universiteit Amsterdam under the supervision of Stefan Paas and Darrell Guder. I could not have asked for two better guides in developing my study, and I remain grateful for their wisdom and cheerful encouragement. In addition, I was deeply blessed along the way with other key missional interlocutors, including (but not limited to) Christopher James, Jonathan Wilson, Priscilla Pope-Levison, Jason Byassee, Keas Keasler, Jeffrey Hoops, Ray Aldred, Paulo Pereira Jr, Joel Thiessen, Robert Fennell, John Bowen, and the Centre for Missional Leadership team at St Andrew's Hall – Albert Chu, Tim Dickau, and Andrea Perrett. This book is stronger because of their keen insights into how Christians are engaging a wider, more diverse, and more secular North American landscape. My thanks as well to the PhD students and scholars at Vrije Universiteit Amsterdam, who were a wonderful community to share my research with and receive feedback from, including at annual symposiums held both in-person and online.

I acknowledge with gratitude the generous support and encouragement (before, during, and after this study) from the board, faculty, and staff at St Andrew's Hall on the University of British Columbia campus where I am privileged to serve as dean. As well, I am thankful to my colleagues across the street at Vancouver School of Theology, where I teach Mission Studies, who have been wonderful conversation partners in this research. I am grateful for the insight of my editor Kyla Madden, the two anonymous peer reviewers whose suggestions improved my work, and the whole team at McGill-Queen's University Press who helped bring this work to print.

Finally, my deepest appreciation to Laura and our children Emily, Jack, and Sadie for their patience and kindness while I was consumed in research and writing over many years. Their ongoing support and care helped fructify my own efforts to learn more about God's activity in the city that we love, and together call home.

WEST COAST MISSION

Lotus Land Life

Examining West Coast Spirituality

INTRODUCTION

It only snows a couple of times a year in Vancouver. Those of us who grew up "back East," as I did on the Canadian Prairies, moved to the West Coast to escape the cold and snow that is so much a part of life in the northern United States and the rest of Canada. In fact, one of the first things I did after moving to Vancouver was visit a local nursery and purchase a palm tree for our tiny back garden. Like planting a flag on the moon, it was my little horticultural statement of arrival in a new and strange land. Vancouver is a place where tropical plants thrive year-round, green grass grows cheerfully in January, and the first buds of spring are instantly uploaded to social media to "encourage" snowbound relations in other parts of Canada. With its laid-back culture and stunning natural beauty, Vancouver has been both envied and mocked by other Canadians over the years, offering the "West Coast paradise" a nickname – Lotus Land.[1]

During the course of writing this book, however, Vancouver had one of those rare snow days when the schools were closed, and I looked out the back window as my beautiful palm tree was bent over, begging for relief like the hurting woman in Luke's gospel.[2] I took my youngest child up to the local hill to toboggan, and while there I struck up a conversation with the man beside me. He remarked on how nice it was for the kids to have a day off school. I agreed and noted how the snow reminded me of growing up in Manitoba, where the temperature regularly dropped to minus forty degrees Celsius, and snow lasted from October through May. The man replied that he was born and raised in Vancouver and never experienced a "real winter." Other pleasantries were exchanged as we pushed our children on their sleds, and at one point he inquired, "So, what school does your daughter go to?" An innocent question. "Lions Gate Christian Academy," I replied not thinking much about it. The other man's body language changed, becoming frostier than the snow falling around us. "Oh," he said, taking a step back and looking puzzled. "So ...," he stuttered, "you're a Christian?" The way he asked the question made Christianity sound like a communicable disease. "Um, yeah, I'm a Christian," I replied with tempered zeal (like a good Presbyterian). He stood there quietly for a moment and continued, "I don't know any Christians. So, what *do* you guys really believe about climate change, anyways?" What began as a simple exercise of taking my daughter tobogganing had now escalated into some off-the-cuff apologetics.

"Well," I replied cautiously, "as Christians we believe God created everything in the Universe, including the earth, and that we are called to be good stewards of creation. As followers of Jesus, we believe in partnering with God to repair the world and are happy to work with anyone, no matter what their faith beliefs might be, to help take care of the planet." Not exactly sparkling evangelism, but it gave me time to continue the conversation and listen as he offered in return the various media-fuelled stereotypes about Christianity not caring about the environment.[3]

The Pacific Northwest region of North America where this study is situated has been described as "rocky soil" for Christian witness, but in that moment with snowflakes swirling around, it felt more like hard, frozen land for sowing the gospel. By the end of the day, however, I knew more about my affable agnostic neighbour, his work as a paramedic, and the soul-crushing feeling of responding to endless overdoses in the city's ongoing opioid crisis. A small window opened for us to find some overlapping consensus on the need for identity, purpose, and meaning in human life, even if we were coming at it from different directions.

By the time my daughter and I packed up and headed home for hot chocolate, I reflected on what has become a normal experience for me as a follower of Jesus in the Pacific Northwest. A long-standing tagline from the local tourist board is "Super, Natural British Columbia," dissecting the divine with a comma in order to emphasize the natural beauty of this West Coast province.[4] It's common to meet neighbours here with little to no working knowledge of Christianity, let alone experience of knowing Christians in the flesh. The Pacific Northwest is a fascinating ecclesiastical and missional Petri dish for those wanting to figure out what Christian witness might look like in the years to come across a more secularized North America. This study of the church in Vancouver hopes to add to that insight.

A SECULAR OR SACRED CITY?

Despite Metro Vancouver being Canada's third-largest city, there is a distinct lack of research addressing the question, "Where is Christianity in Vancouver going now that it is a minority belief system within the broader culture?"[5] Vancouver, British Columbia, statistically reports "no religion" as the number one "religious identity." This is consistent with the broader Pacific Northwest region of North America called Cascadia, which includes the area of study conducted by Christopher James in his examination of church plants in Seattle, Washington.[6]

This urban ethnographic research is conversant with James's research by discovering how Christian communities in Vancouver (from a minority position of influence) are engaging this rapidly changing, globalizing context while helping people establish and deepen their Christian identity.[7] This book has significant differences from James's work, however, including a move beyond church plants. It studies broader Christian initiatives such as established congregations and so-called para-church agencies and explores the distinctives of the Canadian context with its British Commonwealth identity and sensitivities. Scholars who study Christianity in both the United States and Canada note similarities and distinctives on both sides of the border. For example, sociologist Sam Reimer argues that evangelicals share a similar subculture in both countries while Canadian evangelicals are more irenic with a higher level of tolerance for difference and working with those of divergent theological expressions.[8] Reimer also notes that Canadians have been "largely unable to sustain national myths of any kind, much less ones that are seen as religiously significant. Issues that divide Canadians do not tend to fall along moral or religious lines but along ethnic and geographic lines."[9]

In addition, this research took place concurrent with the study by Paul Bramadat at the University of Victoria and his colleagues, published as *Religion at the Edge* in 2022.[10] That work, however, had a broader scope than my own research in focusing on a larger region (all of Cascadia/Pacific Northwest rather than just the city of Vancouver) and a multi-faith approach (that included Christianity).

Valuable insights from that research are engaged later in this study, as are the models of Christian witness developed in James's work. Similar to James's project, this research recognizes that often standard secularization theories describe secularization as a sort of force of nature in the West, something that "happens" to religious people. Instead, believing that religious people are not passive, this study asks: What strategies are Christians actively developing that interact with the broader secular culture and provide evidence of a fulsome soteriology, foster spiritual maturity, encourage Christian witness, enact social justice, and partner with other community organizations for the welfare of the city?[11] These "thick descriptions"[12] go beyond the study of simple conversion behaviour to help understand the context of Christian communities regarding identity and mission, the cultivation of spirituality, the strength of ecumenical relations, and the impact of the Christian community's witness on the broader, secular context of twenty-first-century Vancouver.[13] As Philip Sheldrake reminds us, urban missiology is essential as the world becomes increasingly urban: "the meaning and future of cities globally is one of the most critical spiritual as well as economic and social issues of our age. Urban environments are where, for most of humanity, the practice of everyday life takes place, either constructively or destructively."[14] This kind of research has been described by scholars as a study of Christianity in "liminal spaces." As Moses Biney, Kenneth Ngwa, and Raimundo Barreto note of Christianity in contemporary urban contexts, "in these porous spaces, faith is often relocated and reinvented, and religious theory and praxis is challenged to go beyond furnishing language that justifies exclusivist claims to contribute to open new horizons for creative conviviality."[15]

In this sense, we are entering into not just a liminal space but also a contested space between Canadian sociologists of religion. For example, Joel Thiessen has recently challenged the more established position of his fellow-Albertan sociologist of religion Reginald Bibby who advocated for a "rational choice theory." Bibby's publications over the years encouraged many Canadian Christians to assume their faith tradition had only to find the right technique (what we might call "tips and tricks" theology) to "tap into" the unending demand of things that religion offers, including "meaning and purpose in life, life after death, a supposed 'God shaped hole' that exists in everyone."[16] Instead, Thiessen notes the challenges facing Christian initiatives in Canada despite their best efforts at more effective organization and missional engagement, citing that Canadians move away from religion for several reasons. From his research, these reasons include the Canadian cultural rejection of exclusivity; the setting aside of religious practice through various life transitions (moving to different regions, building a family or career, etc.); the commonly accepted understanding that faith is an individual "choice"; a perceived sense that Canadians are "too busy" for religious expression or it is not a good use of time; the ever-present problem of scandals and hypocrisy within religious institutions; intellectual disagreement with doctrine; interpersonal tension through negative experiences with religious institutions; and the severing of social ties.[17]

CHRISTENDOM'S FAILING GRADE

When Vancouver was incorporated as a city in 1886 (changing its name from Granville), there was already a small, active Christian presence meeting in homes and chapels. At that time the British colony's capital was further east in New Westminster, where the oldest churches were established, with ministers from that community often providing worship and pastoral care sporadically to the people living in the township of Granville. With incorporation in 1886 and the completion of the Canadian Pacific Railway terminus in Vancouver shortly thereafter, the new city grew quickly, and larger places of worship were erected. Homer Street Methodist Church opened in 1889 while St Andrew's Presbyterian Church on West Georgia Street was built in 1890. Christ Church Cathedral (Anglican) was built in 1894, and five hundred metres east the Roman Catholics purchased land and laid the cornerstone of Our Lady of the Holy Rosary in 1898, dedicating it in 1900 and declaring it a cathedral in 1916.

Growth in both the number of church buildings and the variety of Christian denominations occurred in the decades following, as both the city of Vancouver matured and the ethnic and spiritual makeup of the area changed with shifting immigration patterns. From Swedish Lutherans building their first church in the Strathcona neighbourhood in 1910 to Ukrainian Catholics establishing Holy Trinity Parish in 1937, the expression of Christian community changed over time.

Traditionally, Christianity was a significant source of social cohesiveness in Canadian villages, towns, and cities as congregations of Latin Western Christendom were planted in partnership with the development of the British, French, and Spanish colonies of North

America. Over the last several decades, however, many studies have
been conducted narrating the disestablishment of the mainline
Protestant churches' influence in North America society, what Diana
Butler Bass calls "cultural displacement"[18] and "detraditionalization."[19] But here in the Pacific Northwest, or Cascadia, some argue
that Christendom was never fully established.

In the 1901 census British Columbians were ten times more likely
than the average Canadian to call themselves atheists or agnostics, or
to state they had no religion. Ever since, British Columbia has had the
highest proportion of Canadians declaring "no religion" of any province.[20] For example, from 2017 to 2019, more than half (53 per cent)
of people born between 1981 and 1996, commonly known as
Millennials, report having no religious affiliation.[21] A common late-
nineteenth-century saying declared that men left God behind when
they crossed the Rocky Mountains into British Columbia.[22] University
of Victoria historian Lynn Marks has carefully documented the lack of
Christendom status or privilege for Christianity in British Columbia
since the arrival of European settlers on the West Coast. In her work,
Infidels and the Damn Churches, Marks describes the irreligion of the
region ranging from those who told census takers they were atheist
or "infidels" actively rejecting God to those who were simply not
involved in a religious institution. She defines irreligion as "beliefs and
activities that are expressive of attitudes of hostility or indifference
towards prevailing religion."[23] Marks cautions applying a secularization approach to British Columbia that assumes that to be secularized
a culture must first be religious. Instead, she argues that compared to
eastern Canada, nineteenth- and early-twentieth-century British
Columbia was never particularly religious in its identity. Essentially,
despite the best efforts (and funding) from Christian denominations
at work in Canada, the attempt to establish a Christendom framework
in British Columbia failed.

This lack of privilege and social power for Christian denominations
continued into the twentieth century, as Mark's fellow–British
Columbian historian Tina Block demonstrated in her work *The Secular
Northwest*. Block reminds us that census data today on both sides of
the border indicates that "no religion" is now the number one religious
identity in the region.[24] Block's historical survey of faith in Cascadia
in the twentieth century found that "Northwest secularity is most
evident in the region's strikingly low levels of involvement in, and
attachment to, formal or organized religion."[25] Angus Reid's recent

polling on religion in Canada confirms that BC is home to the highest proportion of non-believers at just over one-quarter (27 per cent).[26]

Today, within both church and academia the dramatic impact of post-Enlightenment secularity in the West is regularly discussed and acknowledged.[27] Secularism has not only manifested as a philosophical and political ideology striving to remove religious symbols, beliefs, and influence from public life but also changed the very nature of the conditions of our understanding of what it means to be human, whether religious or irreligious, living and thinking in what Charles Taylor calls "the immanent frame."[28] In his work *A Secular Age*, Taylor asks the question: "What does it mean to say that we live in a secular age?" He narrates three distinct ways in which secularism may be understood today. First, secularity refers to the removal of God from the public square noting the declining influence of religious institutions. Second, secularism emerges as an ideology as fewer people engage in religious practice and commitment to formal religious institutions. Society becomes less influenced by religious thought and citizens become less committed to religious observance through institutions in these first two scenarios. Third, Taylor suggests that secularity is a total change in our experience of the world. Not only do faith institutions no longer hold sway, nor are they well attended, but also people, whether or not they are "believers," think in secular ways. In other words, people live as if there is no divine agency in the world. In missiologist Stefan Paas's description of this reality, "the secularization of Western culture (in the sense of the immanentization of our worldviews) is not merely an outside force to be challenged through the mission of faithful Christians; secularization is also part of the Christian life itself."[29] Taylor argues that in the West, "the shift to secularity ... consists ... of a move from a society where belief in God is unchallenged and indeed, unproblematic, to one in which it is understood to be one option among others, and frequently not the easiest to embrace."[30]

Recent research by Canadian scholars Stuart Macdonald and Brian Clarke has explored the steps of mainline Christian denominational decline in the final decades of the last century. In *Leaving Christianity: Changing Allegiances in Canada since 1945*, Macdonald and Clarke describe the contemporary context this way: "Decline in Christian affiliation, membership, and participation started in the 1960s and has picked up pace rapidly since then. This trend is likely to continue and, indeed, accelerate as an increasing portion of the country's

population – among youth especially – have never been exposed to
Christianity ... In short, Canadian society is entering into a new era,
a post-Christian era. The end of Christendom ... occurred in the closing decades of the twentieth century, as churches lost their social
power and their place in the nation's cultural fabric."[31]

Noting the loss of the baby boomer generation's participation in
local churches, *Leaving Christianity* acknowledges that today
there are many Canadians who have left the church as well as an
increasing number in what is commonly called the Millennial (born
between 1981 and 1996) and iGen or Gen Z (born 1997 to 2012)
generations for whom the Christian message and participation within
a faith community is unknown.[32] Macdonald and Clarke call this
the distinction between being "de-churched and non-churched." They
suggest that "the de-churched are those who at some point in their
lives attended church but now no longer do so. The non-churched
have never attended except perhaps for a funeral or wedding of a
friend or relation." To them Christianity is, in the words of the
Church of England's report *Mission Shaped Church*, "an utterly
foreign culture."[33] Macdonald and Clarke conclude: "First, people
are not only leaving churches; they are leaving Christianity. And many
of them have no interest in returning. Second, an increasing and
significant proportion of the population has never had any first-hand
experience of organized religion."[34]

By the time I began the research for this book in 2018, concluding
the project in 2022, I was able to identify 277 Christian initiatives
(churches and agencies) within the boundaries of the city of Vancouver.
As mentioned earlier, according to the Government of Canada's 2021
National Household Survey conducted by Statistics Canada,
Christianity has a minority status in the city of Vancouver compared
to the larger category of residents describing themselves as having "no
religion."[35] Of the 650,380 respondents in 2021,[36] 362,925 reported
"no religion and secular perspectives" compared to 194,365 Christians
of various denominations – including nearly half (94,425) who identified as Catholic. Into this ethnographic mix, it is important to note
the presence of other world religions. For example, in Vancouver there
were more than twice as many Buddhists (26,245) as Anglicans
(11,970) and almost five times as many Jews (11,675) as Presbyterians
(2,390); twice as many Sikhs (16,535) as United Church (8,575); and
seven times as many Muslims (17,910) as Pentecostals (2,465).

Having never fully enjoyed the Christendom privileges present for the rest of Canadians "back East," Christian witness in Vancouver is in flux. This book explores where Christianity in Vancouver is going now that it is a minority belief system within the broader culture. Indeed, given that the dominant culture is no longer even nominally Christian, interest focuses on how Christian initiatives, from a minority perspective, engage in mission, understand their theology and spirituality within this context, and organize themselves in this diverse and cosmopolitan city.[37]

The lack of a Christendom heritage has left many church leaders struggling with how best to respond as a Christian community finding itself in a culture that is rapidly changing. As one leader wrote to me, "we are unclear how to reach our community in an effective way. We have some activities but struggle to leverage those into opportunities to communicate the Gospel."[38] Another church leader in East Vancouver described his neighbourhood in an email to me saying, "Vancouver is an isolated place for many people. People are struggling with issues in their personal lives and families on their own. They seem generally suspicious of the church. Building significant relationships in our communities allows us to share the good news of Jesus and welcome people into Kingdom discipleship."[39] To that end, British Columbian theologian Jonathan Wilson claims that a distinctive gift of Christianity is that the gospel is an invitation to move from fragmented lives to participating in the church as beloved community. Drawing on decades of work studying philosopher Alasdair MacIntyre, Wilson argues that "the people of God have good news for the people of Cascadia – including ourselves. In Jesus Christ the purpose of the cosmos – all creation – has been revealed and realized and we are invited to participate in the formation of that beloved community. This news requires us to change our minds and our lives – to repent of the attempt to be our own creators. Only then may our fragmentation begin to be healed as we participate in God's plan to 'bring unity to all things in heaven and on earth under Christ' (Eph 1:10)."[40] Will there be evidence of this "beloved community" in Vancouver initiatives that is non-competitive and, according to Lisa Slayton and Herb Kolbe, evidence of Christian communities reflecting the mutual, self-giving love of the triune God? They ask of individuals and churches starting new ministries in urban areas where ministries already exist: "Why is partnering not our first thought and response in these instances? We must learn to seek collaboration in urban ministry ... setting aside ego and join what God may already be doing through others."[41]

In addition, recent research on churches in the region has discovered vibrant pan-Asian congregations that offer an alternative narrative, that unsettles the assumption that Christianity is something that British Columbians' grandparents left behind when they crossed the Rocky Mountains.[42] Will Vancouver further challenge the broader linear narrative of a secularizing modernity that sociologist Anna Strhan has named as "increasingly problematized" whereby we assume that urbanization naturally leads to secularization?[43] As recent research by Canadian sociologists determined, projections are that immigration to Canada in the years ahead will be primarily from Asian countries. They argue that "if current trends continue, they [immigrants] will be almost equally divided between people who are Catholic, Muslim, and those who have no religion. Typically, Catholic immigrants are more conservative than those born in Canada in their theological and social beliefs."[44]

As we move towards fieldwork exploring these questions of organizational culture, there is a curiosity about "what the Spirit is animating" in the Vancouver context when it comes to translating the Christian faith and building Christian communities. As Reginald Bibby recently noted, "seen from the vantage point of the organizational analyst, religious groups are like businesses trying to make headway in the religious market. Some succeed, some fail. But, nevertheless, the market continues to exist, awaiting new and more effective entries."[45]

WHITHER WEST COAST CHRISTIANITY?

The popular image in the Canadian media, especially on the secular West Coast, is that Christianity is in decline numerically, a fading part of colonial history from Euro-tribal churches once planted across the country during two centuries of nation building. For example, the media have recently profiled the Anglican Church of Canada as declining to the point of zero membership by the year 2040,[46] while researchers note that the United Church of Canada closes a congregation each week and Canada's largest Christian denomination, the Roman Catholic Church, has closed four hundred and fifty parishes, nearly one-fifth of its congregations.[47]

Others who profile religion in the Canadian media have suggested that the impact of closed church buildings during COVID-19 will hasten the decline of Christianity.⁴⁸ This assumption that church decline is inevitable finds its way into various congregations, judicatories, and seminary classrooms where people ask, "Is Christianity dying in Canada?" Therefore, this book echoes Christian Scharen's work that seeks a theory that "emerges from problems that arise in trying to understand a particular field or social context within a particular research project."⁴⁹ This book seeks to understand in a more fulsome manner the ways in which missional engagement is performed by churches (Christian initiatives)⁵⁰ in Vancouver, how they are motivated (theological constructions of the city, missional theology, and spirituality), and which cultural and organizational forms do these performances assume. After all, secular Vancouverites often speak of their city in spiritual and even soteriological terms: one neighbour, while putting out their recycling, told me in confessional tones that "living in Vancouver is like being in paradise"; another said that a regular hike on the North Shore Mountains "saves me from despair and gives me hope." Later, we will hear from other researchers in the region, like Paul Bramadat, who have named this awe for the environment as "reverential naturalism," leading James Wellman Jr and Katie Corcoran to argue that this "nature religion" is the dominant civil religion in Cascadia.⁵¹ This connection between place, nature, and spirituality is strong in the region, prompting me to quip from time to time, "the hardest thing about preaching heaven in Vancouver is most people think they are *already there*."

In addition, I am curious about this assumption that Christianity is declining and wonder also if perhaps *Christianity is changing* in a way not yet recognized by either the broader media or the declining historic churches once planted as franchises of European Christendom. As Reginald Bibby, a Canadian sociologist of religion, said rather bluntly in his latest publication: "Let me be pointed and emphatic: it's time that we stopped navel gazing and pontificating about how growing secularity is going to virtually eliminate religion in Canada. It hasn't happened, and it's never going to happen. Likewise, let's be perfectly clear about the nature of religious polarization. Religion is also never going to eradicate secular inclinations. My central point is that pro-religious and no-religious inclinations – along with the choice of the religious middle – have always been with us, even if they haven't received the publicity they deserve."⁵²

Could it be that the "face of Christianity" is being remade in this city due to the large immigration of new residents from across Asia, many of whom arrive with a Christian identity or adopt one soon after arrival? North American missiologists such as Soong-Chan Rah have been leaning into these questions, asking what it means to be the church in the midst of changing demographics and a transforming culture.[53] Afe Adogame and James Spickard have even identified seven different patterns of global Christian migration to new contexts that remind us that Christian initiatives in the West are often difficult to spot from a Eurocentric perspective.[54] Therefore, this book addresses the following question: *"How are Christians in Vancouver today, as a minority expression of the majority secular population, organizing their communities, shaping their beliefs, and expressing themselves in mission?"*

The intention is to address the above question by describing, through ethnographic research, the cross-cultural and culture-specific trends of Christianity in the city of Vancouver by producing rich qualitative data, and identifying trends and types in Christian organization, community formation, spirituality, culture(s), and mission. The resulting evidence-based thick descriptions of Christian initiatives in Vancouver intend to make a modest contribution to complement existing research of religion in the West, including the normative aspect of best practices for those Christian and other religious leaders looking for viable strategies to improve their mission.

ETHNOGRAPHIC MISSIOLOGY

This book reflects an urban ethnographic approach to the study of Christian communities in Vancouver. Ethnographic theology is a relatively recent development in academia, beginning in the twentieth century as practical theologians and social scientists studied urban Christianity with the rise of the social gospel. While a more recent area of study, ethnographic theology is best situated within the more established field of practical theology.

Practical theology is critical, theological reflection on the practices of the church as they interact with the practices of the world, with a view to ensuring faithful participation in the continuing mission of the triune God.[55] Pete Ward notes that practical theology takes seriously that knowledge of God is distinct from other kinds of knowledge (mathematics, for example, that you can learn by sitting down and studying multiplication tables) and that, epistemologically, Christians take seriously that God is participatory in nature. Thus, for Ward, the practice of theology is sharing in the life of God.[56] Richard Osmer notes that of all the fields of theology, practical theology gives the most attention to studying and learning from the present context, as well as even transforming it, all the while taking human experience seriously.[57] John Swinton and Harriet Mowat remind us that practical theology is unlike the social sciences in that there is an end or telos that transcends all particular forms of action. This telos constitutes the primary purpose and meaning of human life, and the eschatological horizon of the practical theology enterprise, as Swinton and Mowat argue, "for the practical theologian action is not merely pragmatic, or problem-solving ... action always has a goal of interacting with situations and challenging practice in order that individuals and communities can be enabled to remain faithful to God and participate in God's mission."[58]

Early forms of urban ethnographic theology in Canada include the work of J.S. Woodsworth, who wrote *Strangers Within our Gates*, and Salem Bland, who authored *The New Christianity*, while in the United States Paul Douglass's 1927 *The Church in the Changing City* gave evidence of Christians paying closer attention to the influence of industrialization and urbanization, and the role of the churches. Congregational studies continued over the next several decades, and in the 1970s Gaylord Noyce's *Survival and Mission for the City Church* noted churches responding to their changing urban environment by focusing on becoming a niche congregation, simply declining, adapting to the changing landscape, or moving out of the neighbourhood altogether. Around this same period Ray Bakke was writing about Christianity in Chicago while teaching church history at McCormick Theological Seminary and pastoring an inner-city congregation. He noted that several challenges were present in urban Christian witness, including the changing nature of demographics, economics, migration, ecclesiastical structure, and lack of adaption as well as funding for urban ministries. Others continued in this development of urban ethnography as a first-hand study of city life. They immersed themselves in the worlds of people about whom they wrote to capture and analyze how Christianity was adapting now that the majority of North Americans live in urban rather than rural settings. A notable urban ethnographic study completed by Nancy Ammerman and her research colleagues in the 1990s was published as *Congregations and Community*. Together, they focused on a diverse set of congregations across the United States in a Lilly Endowment–funded project that examined three broad dimensions of congregational life: resources, structures of authority, and congregational culture.[59]

In Canada, sociologist Joel Thiessen and a team at Ambrose University's Flourishing Congregations Institute has published recent research interviewing leaders in Catholic, mainline Protestant, and conservative Protestant churches. The researchers took an inductive approach to the question of what helps a congregation flourish, noting "no congregation flourishes in every way" and that "flourishing is best thought of as being along a dynamic and fluid spectrum (suffering, struggling, thriving) or as a series of lifecycles."[60] Working with the data, Thiessen has summarized the key markers across ecclesiastical traditions that indicate congregational flourishing in Canada (see figure 1.1).

Thiessen is quick to note, however, that the indicators for flourishing are not evenly distributed across each congregation and that the research suggests that "certain theological traditions stress some dimensions more than they do others."[61] Thiessen and his team stress the importance of data from the Canadian context (to which this study of Vancouver contributes), noting that the cultural milieu is "drastically different" for "how churches are perceived and how they ultimately operate."[62]

For many years, Montreal-based missiologist Glenn Smith has been studying how Christians interact with their multicultural, multi-faith neighbours for the sake of the common good. Barna Group defines this "common good" attempt at overlapping consensus with diverse neighbours as "the flourishing or well-being of the sum total of communal life in a given place."[63] Through his urban research, Smith has developed twelve indicators of a Christian vision for a transformed city in Canada that connect with the overall themes of creation, society, urban community, church reconciliation, evangelism and service, justice, and stewardship.[64] Smith, who is professor of Urban Missiology at the Institut de Théologie pour la Francophonie in Montreal, argues that the twelve indicators represent God's concern for all of life, beginning with the congregation that embodies shalom and reconciliation. These communities then demonstrate the good news in their neighbourhoods in word and deed. They are also deeply concerned about justice and forgiveness in society, and act in partnership with others as stewards for the whole created order.[65]

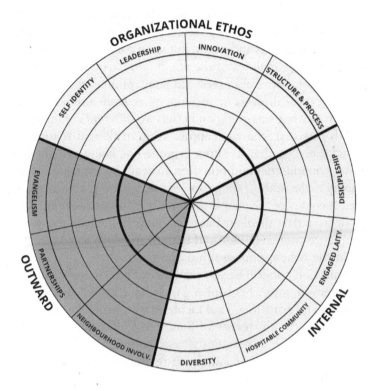

Figure 1.1 Key indicators of congregational flourishing

In the past two decades, scholars such as Christian Scharen have been further developing this urban ethnographic approach, acknowledging that there is too often a gap between ethnography, namely qualitative research, and ecclesiology, with its normative theological focus. Scharen names the bridging of this divide as a priority of his pastoral and scholarly life. He writes that "in order for scholarship about the church to be most helpful to the church ... rapprochement between empirical and theological understandings of the church ought to be encouraged in such a way that the actual life of the church is attended to, thought through theologically, and thereby strengthened (one hopes) for more faithful witness."[66] This bridging of the empirical and theological understandings of the church is a delicate balance as researchers are often professed Christians within academia who seek both a descriptive and normative analysis of urban Christianity today. For Scharen, the desire to further develop this ethnographic/urban approach was nurtured by his work with the Lutheran Volunteer Corps in Philadelphia that forced him to straddle between a Franciscan-based ministry to the homeless and a local Lutheran congregation that seemed detached from the realities of the community around it.[67] His early experimentation with field notes and later training in sociology and anthropology in California helped him move from a thin to a thicker description of what was going on in the two different communities of faith. It also assisted Scharen in appreciating an alternative form to the scholastic theology that he often critiqued as being detached from particular communities and practices. Instead, by applying social science theory to the study of congregations, Scharen was able to articulate the lived theology of the people more clearly "as an emerging form of formal or secondary theology but much more immediately responsible to the practice contexts of life and faith from which it spoke."[68]

Within the urban ethnographic approach, three separate recent North American publications by professors Paul Lichterman, Natalie Wigg-Stevenson, and Christopher James have gained recognition in both church and academia. Paul Lichterman, a professor of sociology and religion at the University of Southern California, engaged in a three-year study of nine religiously based community service agencies in the midwestern city of Lakeburg responding to social welfare reform in the community. Lichterman was curious about what being involved in local church life meant to religious people and whether they would bring religion into the civic arena.[69] Lichterman acknowledges early on that he is unconvinced by the traditional social capital assumptions that people make regarding social agencies (including religiously based ones) and their impact on the cohesion of society. Drawing on insights from Alexis de Tocqueville, Jane Addams, and John Dewey, he notes that many of the nine religious agencies struggled to create external ties due, in part, to the powerful customs of interaction within the agency. Lichterman called overcoming this inward focus "bridging," which he defined as "a routinized relationship that a civic group has to individuals or groups that it perceives as outside the group."[70] He identified examples of this "bridging" where deeper connections were made with external groups when the religious agencies developed more robust reflective and critical practices that engaged the reality of the agency vis-à-vis the surrounding groups and institutions. Successful agencies went beyond religious doctrine, institutional resources, or political preferences and were able to learn new ways of forming group identity in light of their neighbour.

Lichterman noted how people of faith reacted differently in the same context and acknowledged that as a sociologist it is better to ask what people do with religion instead of what religion makes people do or be: "I learned that religion makes people neither civic-minded nor anti-civic minded. Rather, people carry religion into different kinds of civic activities with very different styles of expressions."[71]

A second study was conducted by Natalie Wigg-Stevenson, an associate professor in contextual education and theology at Emmanuel College, Toronto. She focused her doctoral work at Vanderbilt University on First Baptist Church in Nashville, Tennessee. Wigg-Stevenson described her ethnographic study as something different than reflection upon Christian community or on Christian practice: "I sought to do theological reflection *in* Christian community *as* Christian practice. I wondered, 'What happens when we bring together every day and academic theologies into a reciprocal conversation? What types of theology can be produced out of their coherence and clash with each other?'"[72] Throughout her work, Wigg-Stevenson explores the question of how ethnographic methods help foster the organic relationship between everyday and academic theologies in order to bolster their shared production of theological knowledge.[73]

Drawing on the work of sociologist Pierre Bourdieu, Wigg-Stevenson acknowledges that to think in terms of a field of study is to think relationally.[74] Her work with Nashville First Baptist Church explored the habitus of the community that she defined as "types of embodied, knowledgeable agency" and how that agency reconfigures "the context that situates it."[75] Acknowledging that her staff position at First Baptist Church placed her in the role of a participant observer, she named her own reflexivity in needing to avoid Bourdieu's caution of leaning too far in the direction of either objectivism or subjectivism with a desire to perform participant objectification.[76] Drawing on Christian Scharen's work, Wigg-Stevenson notes that her goal of an ethnographic/urban approach to congregational study is theological epistemology. She seeks to understand how theology is produced and "how might it be or ought to be produced when the organic overlap between every day and academic forms of theological knowledge is made apparent and nurtured."[77] For Wigg-Stevenson, the ethnographic/urban theologian's approach is not one where information is simply mined out of a field of study, but rather one of nurturing "the places where every day Christians and academic theologians are already cocreating theological knowledge."[78]

While Wigg-Stevenson was working on her urban ethnography research in Nashville, Christopher James was conducting a different study focused on church plants in Seattle, Washington. James defines the lens of practical theology that he uses to study new Christian worshipping communities in Seattle as a "missional practical ecclesiological reflection" that moves through four stages of description, interpretation, evaluation, and proposals.[79] James describes his field of study in Seattle as urban, progressive, technological, and post-Christian. Through a New Seattle Church Survey, he was able to interpret four models of new Christian communities: Great Commission Team, Household of the Spirit, New Community, and Neighborhood Incarnation.[80]

Acknowledging that churches are diverse, complex, and both sociocultural and theological realities, he offers a normative response to the question of church plant models in Seattle. These include communities of new Christian faith that are embracing local identity and mission; cultivating embodied, experiential, everyday spirituality; engaging community life as a means of witness and formation; prioritizing hospitality as a cornerstone practice; and discovering ecclesial vitality in a diverse ecclesial ecology.[81] His project is about "helping Christian communities fulfill their vocations as witnesses to the good news of Jesus Christ in rapidly evolving Western contexts."[82]

James acknowledges the impact of missional theology on the ethnographic/urban approach to congregational study, calling it "one of the most important theological developments of the twentieth century."[83] Describing missional theology as "Trinitarian theology in which God is known as a missionary God," James notes theologian Darrell Guder's influence in making missional theology also Christocentric through an emphasis upon "incarnational mission" rooted in the life, ministry, death, and resurrection of Jesus.[84] James explores the four typologies of church plants identified in Seattle, assessing them for strengths and weaknesses through the lens of missional theology, and in addition characterizes the renewed practices of each model. First, Great Commission Teams, which exhibit deep evangelical roots and seek to connect for conversion. Second, Household of the Spirit communities, which have charismatic or Pentecostal roots and seek to draw participants into enthusiasm of the Spirit at work in the world. Third, New Community church plants, which tend to have mainline denominational roots and have a high degree of tolerance for ambiguity and mystery in their framing of the

Christian faith. Fourth, Neighborhood Incarnation church plants, which draw on a mix of all these approaches but keep their focus on being a blessing in their immediate geographic neighbourhoods. Concluding with practical wisdom for Christian witness and church planting in a post-Christendom West, James acknowledges that the dominant narrative that the church is dying is incorrect; rather, the church is changing.[85] James's urban ethnographic approach in Seattle significantly influenced the research in this book exploring Christian witness in the city of Vancouver. *Church Planting in Post-Christian Soil* sparked interest in whether similar dynamics were at play two hundred kilometres north along Interstate 5 in British Columbia within the larger Christian community, not just amongst church plants. To that question, we now turn our attention.

The research in this book is grounded in an urban ethnographic approach in the field of congregational studies, without limiting the research to congregations alone. It employs qualitative methods, including observation; analysis of texts and documents; and interviews, recordings, and transcription.[86] The intention behind the method was to develop reliable evidence-based thick descriptions from studying the data of Christian forms of institutionalization to complement existing research in the field of practical theology, using ethnographic research and theological reflection to offer proposals for analyzing and improving current ecclesial and missional practices in the city of Vancouver.[87]

The methodology in this book acknowledges Christian Scharen's concern regarding the need to hold together empirical and theological understandings of the church through research by professing Christians who seek both a descriptive and normative analysis of urban Christianity today. Therefore, the methodology attends not only to ecclesiology that can be defined as "a theological discipline that seeks to understand and define the church" but also missiology defined as "a theological discipline that seeks to understand and define both the creating and redeeming works of God in the world ."[88] This research focuses on three key areas.

First, a focus on mission, with the desire to discover and study the various strategies and efforts of engagement with the city made by these diverse Christian initiatives in order to have an impact on the wider urban community around them. Second, a focus on theology and spirituality, exploring the motivating beliefs present in these Christian initiatives. Third, a focus on culture, whereby the organizational forms and styles of the particular expressions of Christian community and action are analyzed.

This work is undertaken acknowledging the shift in the last several decades within both mission studies and sociology profiling the role of Christian communities in the secular West, including immigrant communities to North America from Africa, Asia and Sourth America.[89] This Vancouver research makes its own contribution in conversation with other North American and international projects, offering a perspective from the Canadian context of both increasing secularity and, due to ongoing immigration, the changing composition of the Christian population in the country. By focusing on Canada's largest Pacific Rim city, the interpretative method of the study is influenced by what David Leong, in his research in nearby Seattle, calls "urban exegesis," or a "structured approach to theological interpretation of the urban context."[90]

METHODOLOGICAL ORIENTATION

Having located this research within the emerging field of ethnographic theology, the following notes some specific methodological aspects of this study. A more fulsome discussion on methodology, including the field guide used in the focus group discussions, is provided in chapter 2. My intention as a researcher was to cast the net as wide as possible to reflect the diverse Christian presence within the city of Vancouver, based on my experience of the church in this region over the last two decades as both a congregational minister and a professor. The decision to select fourteen sites was an attempt to visit as diverse an ecclesial expression as possible, while still making the sample a reasonable enough size to work with the data. For example, I had debated whether to visit sixteen sites and add house churches to the study but felt the sample was large enough so left that research for a future project.[91] As noted later in chapter 2, I convened a focus group of pastors to help work through aspects of the initial stages of my research. The pastors represented a wide variety of the categories that ended up framing my fieldwork (e.g., neighbourhood focused, church plants, etc.). From this group, I followed up with those who indicated a willingness to participate further in the research, and selected congregations in categories that demonstrated both similarities to and differences from each other. So, for example, in the church plant category, I selected two newly established congregations that meet only a few blocks from each other, both of which seek to reach downtown residents (similarity). One church plant has taken a significant decision against the theological convictions of their denomination to be pro-inclusion regarding human sexuality (which resulted in the judicatory removing them from fellowship); the other church plant defines itself as Anglican but is a breakaway from the mainline denomination in order to maintain a traditional view of human sexuality (difference). Having been active in the small Vancouver Christian community for two decades, I knew most, but not all, of the clergy leaders of these communities. This relational connection and high degree of trust helped gain access to the ministry sites since clergy often serve as gatekeepers.

Once the sites were selected, I explored each initiative's online presence, reviewing the websites, social media platforms, and, on average, two to four blogs or podcasts per site. The content analysis for these online reviews included the look and feel of the website (traditional, text or image dominant, etc.); whether the initiative's purpose and mission were clearly described; whether the theological convictions were evident (traditional, progressive, etc.), including positions on human sexuality; denominational affiliation (if any); representation of leadership, including whether an accountability structure was clear (how it is governed); and how (if at all) the city of Vancouver was represented online (e.g., a focus on a particular neighbourhood). As Mary Clark Moschella notes, "digital platforms clearly extend the reach of research in practical theology" and "ethnography is gradually expanding to take this dimension of human social life into account."[92]

Next, I arranged a "walking interview" with the ministry leader. By walking interview, I mean that I arranged first to meet the clergyperson at their church building. After a tour of the facility, I invited them to take me on a walk in their neighbourhood, describing its unique characteristics and articulating how their congregation connected with their neighbours. The walk normally ended at a coffee shop of the leader's choice where we sat with a latte (and occasional high-calorie sweet treat) and discussed their ministry context further. The average time of these walking interviews was one hour and thirty minutes. After each meeting, I immediately wrote down my observations and kept detailed field notes of each conversation.

At the conclusion of each walking interview, I asked the ministry leader to put me in touch by email with five to seven members of their congregation who might be willing to participate in a focus group conversation. I asked each ministry leader to try to make the focus group participant invitation list as representative of their whole faith community as possible regarding age, gender, and ethnic diversity. Once provided with the email addresses of possible participants, I contacted the individuals and arranged a time to meet with each group on Zoom. (For more details on the focus group interviews, see chapter 2).

Finally, I included a participant observation exercise in worship for each of the sites. The content analysis for each participant observation exercise included attending to the architecture and layout of the space, the liturgical furniture, religious symbols and art, the use (or not) of media and technology such as projection equipment, a general sense of participants (age, ethnicities, gender, dress, etc.), how long the service (and sermon/message) lasted, order of the worship service, music, main focus of the teaching time, summary of prayer content, and what happened after the service, including whether there was a gathering time or coffee hour.

Following the pattern of Christopher James in his study of church plants in Seattle where ministry leaders declined anonymity,[93] so too in my Vancouver research, the actual names of ministry leaders and their initiative appears in the research. Focus group participants were identified only by the particular initiative and not by their individual names as detailed in the consent form. As a researcher I debated whether there should be anonymity for all involved but felt that since the Christian community is so small in Vancouver even the description of the online presence would "give away" which community I was profiling. For example, if I said a church plant in Vancouver that decided to adopt a LGBTQI[94] inclusion position and was removed by their denomination, most Christians in Vancouver would know I was describing Artisan Church and that Nelson Boschman was the ministry leader at the time. Therefore, the rationale was to identify the leader and the initiative but maintain anonymity for focus group participants who would not be well known to a broader public.[95]

AN INVITATION ON A JOURNEY

With that background established, we are ready to move forward. You are invited, through the chapters ahead, to journey across Vancouver to discern and distill the various ways that Christians are gathering and serving this post-Christendom city in which they live, work, and play. From the hipster coffee shops of the Kitsilano neighbourhood to the leafy green streets of the West End to the hard-scrabble sidewalks of the Downtown Eastside, we will listen carefully to the voices of those who seek a credible Christian witness on the West Coast.

Chapter 2 prepares us for the study of Christian communities in the city by grounding our upcoming ethnographic work in various research categories and establishing a field guide for interviews. In chapter 3 we get out on the streets – walking with pastors, attending worship services, and sitting with focus groups to get a better sense of how Christians are living out their faith and connecting with others in Vancouver. Chapter 4 attends to the data generated from the fieldwork, sorts through our findings, and identifies seven clusters of meaning. Based on those reflections, chapter 5 describes five normative outcomes that have broader application to those studying trends in urban religious practice across North America.

While the default story continues to be one of Christianity's decline on the West Coast, with Christians now a smaller proportion of the general population,[96] the upcoming chapters narrate the steps that Christians are taking to form community and share their faith with others in a diverse and distinct context. The research offers a minority report of sorts, highlighting the presence and impact of Christian communities in the city offering their West Coast witness from an ancient faith tradition to their secular neighbours who also call this "paradise" home.

2

Packing a Bag

Preparing for a Journey through
Vancouver's Churches

The subway platform was crowded with the usual assortment of Vancouver's rush hour commuters. It was a chilly December morning, and after years of planning, construction, and delays, TransLink, Metro Vancouver's transportation agency, was officially opening its fourth Skytrain route known as the Evergreen Line. I stood waiting instead for the Canada Line, built a few years earlier for the 2010 Winter Olympics. I watched an older transit employee changing the signs in the station, to accurately reflect this latest growth in the subway system. I smiled and greeted the man as he removed the plastic wrap off a new sign, his voice barely audible above the cacophony of sounds in the station. "I started working this job thirty years ago when the first Skytrain opened for Expo 86," he said, pausing to reach for a screwdriver. "Since then, these maps of the transit system keep changing *all the time*. It's hard to keep up." He paused, thinking for a moment, and then continued, "In a few years I suppose someone else will be changing these signs all over again, when we finally get that SkyTrain built to the university." He stopped, looking pensive, and then continued, "All this change. You know, making maps must be hard, but *making sense of them is harder.*"

This book is a study of Christianity in the city of Vancouver at the beginning of the third decade of the twenty-first century, with a focus on determining how diverse expressions of the Christian religion in Canada's third-largest city are engaging in and responding to a multi-cultural, Pacific Rim–influenced, and highly secularized context.[1] While making a map of Christianity in Vancouver is important, as the TransLink employee noted, *making sense* of a map is both more challenging and rewarding. As University of British Columbia urban geographer David Ley reminds us regarding cities, "in the quest to understand society, things are not always as they appear; causes and consequences may be concealed; subtle explanations may on the surface seem implausible."[2] This hermeneutical task of interpreting the map of Christianity in Vancouver is based on certain assumptions and curiosities that we name and explore in this chapter.

MAKING MAPS, MAKING SENSE

Before beginning any journey, one must set out their plans, consult a map, and pack accordingly. Therefore, before we begin the exploration of fourteen Christian communities in Vancouver through the fieldwork that follows in chapter 3, we first name our curiosities about what we might see and prepare both a method for our journey and questions for engaging Christians in the study along the way. Just as one might stand in the travel section of a bookstore with information about various cities and countries arrayed on the shelf before them, we are reminded that a journey to a specific place can never be generic. Rather, this intensive visitation of Vancouver will reveal the particularities and peculiarities of Christian life and witness in the city, shaped in good part by the people and places of this West Coast urban setting. Therefore, in making our map of Vancouver we recognize that the city is distinct from other regions of Canada, in part, due to its geography, climate, and culture. Raymond Madden notes that "the relationships between humans and places are complex and multi-layered. Humans are place-makers and places make humans."[3] Nicholas Wolterstorff describes the particular challenge that an urban place or context means for human beings when he writes that "the tragedy of modern urban life is not only that so many in our cities are oppressed and powerless, but also that so many have nothing surrounding them in which any human being could possibly take sensory delight."[4] Vancouver, however, does not fit this assumption and instead is known for its stunning natural beauty and postcard-perfect images of a clean, urban context. Hemmed in by snow-capped mountains to the north, the Pacific Ocean to the west, and the United States border only forty kilometres away to the south, Vancouver holds a unique geographic space. As one of the few regions in Canada without significant snowfall in the winter, vegetation is different on the West Coast: year-round hues of deep-green and tropical flowers of vibrant colour; palm trees swaying in the wind pointing west towards Hawaii or south to California where they seem more naturally to belong. Health and fitness are prized among the local population where year-round outdoor activities keep locals busy, from Vancouver-based Lululemon's yoga in the park to skiing on the North Shore Mountains to cycling the city's designated bike lanes or strolling the Stanley Park Seawall while sipping a latte in this coffee-culture town. More than once, you will hear people casually referring to the fact that they are "living in paradise," revealing a glimpse into the soteriological doxa of this so-called secular city.[5]

In the process of developing our map of Vancouver, it is helpful to name four initial curiosities that shape our understanding of the city and its people: witness and language, theological identity and the secular context, bridging and diversity, and missional rhetoric vs. missional practice.

Witness and Language

In preparation for the fieldwork, a curiosity developed regarding how Vancouver Christians articulated their faith convictions in the larger, more secular context outside Christian gatherings, such as in the workplace and in social gatherings. James Wellman Jr and Katie Corcoran have noted in their research that Cascadians typically respond to organized religion with "indifference and occasionally with hostility," creating a challenge for Christians in the region where "people rarely talk about church in public venues, or even among acquaintances, making it difficult for individuals within specific Christian traditions to discuss their faith with others."[6] Connected to this question is how Christian initiatives of various kinds equip their members for this kind of "faith talk" in a more secular Vancouver context. For example, Peter Beyer and Rubina Ramji argue that in Canada, unlike the United States, there is a low level of what "one might call religious aggressiveness, what some might want to call 'competitiveness'" and instead, from a Canadian cultural perspective, "pushing one's religion publicly or even to be too open about showing it" would generally be considered impolite.[7] If this is true, then how are Christian initiatives in Vancouver equipping their members for this kind of relational connection with their neighbours in the city? Here, there is an echo of R. Drew Smith's question of effective urban ministries: "Are the necessary leaders and training opportunities in place to nurture and facilitate faith perspectives and innovation contributing to more robust and reciprocal church and community relations?"[8] So, for example, if the broader secular culture no longer helps form Christian identity, how are Christian initiatives themselves (internally) shaping and equipping their members for Christian witness and practice when out in the broader community? Are they proactively equipping members for a speech act, like St James Church in London, England, that sociologist of religion Anna Strhan studied? In that context an emphasis was placed not upon good works but rather a privileging of "verbal mission" bound up with a stress on the importance of public speaking about faith "as part of a narrative emphasizing the de-Christianization of Britain."[9] And even if members of Vancouver Christian initiatives are confident in their Christian identity, do they bear similarity to those church members interviewed by Tanya Luhrmann in the United States who told others in the community they were Christian and believed in God, yet everyone "uses expressions that acknowledge an acute consciousness that their belief has a complicated relationship to the everyday world in which they live?"[10]

Theological Identity and the Secular Context

A further curiosity as we create our map of Vancouver and move towards fieldwork is exploring how Christians, as a minority population in the larger secular city of Vancouver, relate to those outside their faith communities and how that shapes their theological understanding and identity. Recent scholarship by University of Victoria historian Lynn Marks suggests that in British Columbia, mainline or liberal Christians have significantly declined and struggled while evangelical and progressive evangelicals thrive since they provide community, especially among young adults.[11] Canadian sociologist of religion Sam Reimer describes evangelicals as "doing relatively well" compared to other Christian groups, but while they are a growing proportion of church-going Christians, "at the same time, they are declining as a proportion of the broader population."[12] How do the Christians in this research, from a wide variety of denominational backgrounds, view the culture outside of their faith communities? Is the city of Vancouver a "dark place" where evil lurks outside the "safety" of the stained-glass sanctuary, or is it perhaps a place of possible revelation, where the natural beauty serves as a link between Creator and creation? In previous research on Vancouver, I have identified the high

value Vancouverites (and those in the broader Cascadian region) place
on the environment, leading Douglas Todd, writing for the *Vancouver
Sun* and the most prominent journalist on religion in the city, to claim
it as a "West Coast cliché" that when people want to find God (however
named), they go to the beach or a forest not to a church. According to
Todd, however loosely faith expression may be observed in Vancouver,
spirituality and nature are inextricably linked in the public's mind,
making a love of the environment Vancouver's "civil religion."[13] As
my Vancouver colleague and leading Indigenous scholar Ray Aldred
notes, "a people closely connected with the earth help define a spiritual
way of living that is thoroughly grounded within the here and now.
This moves spirituality and perhaps 'religion' out of the category of
the private inner world and into the public real world. Indigenous
peoples have this 'earthly' spirituality that is situated in the land and
is simply living in a good way in all my relationships."[14]

Patrick Keifert's research with congregations serves as an illustration
of where urban congregations flourishing in post-Christendom are
creating community and connecting it to the central spiritual energies
of the congregation. Keifert writes that "rather than presume community, they actively do community development by attending to their
own character (ethos) in relationship to the gospel (logos) and the
audiences they seek to serve in mission (pathos)."[15] Christian Smith
argues that "collective identity is socially constructed through inter-
group distinctions marked by cultural boundaries," but how porous
are those boundaries and are these initiatives organizing themselves to
be more like a bridge to the wider culture or more of a holy huddle?[16]
Or to use Smith's preferred language, borrowed from Peter Berger,[17] if
we have moved away from the sacred canopy due to secularism, many
religious actors (and initiatives) now have only a "sacred umbrella" to
huddle under. As Smith argues, "in the pluralistic, modern world,
people don't need macro-encompassing sacred cosmoses to maintain
their religious beliefs. They only need 'sacred umbrellas,' small, por-
table, accessible relational worlds – religious reference groups – 'under'
which their beliefs can make complete sense."[18] Canadian sociologist
of religion Sam Reimer names this challenge the "age of self-spirituality," noting the shift over the last several generations from external
authority to internal authority (legitimate power) whereby individuals
choose their behaviours and beliefs, deciding who they will be and how
they will identify. No longer defined by religious beliefs and practices
prescribed by religious authorities, "beliefs, practices, and identities

are more fluid and contested, as people rethink their beliefs in light of new attachments and changing priorities."[19] Reimer observes that this turn towards "an internal locus of authority" does not mean that cultural influences have less effect, as people are still influenced by peer pressure and societal norms; rather, it means that legitimacy now resides within the individual rather than an institution.[20]

Bridging and Diversity (Boundary Crossing)

Further developing our map of Vancouver includes curiosities in the fieldwork that raise questions regarding how Christians in Vancouver relate to those outside their own faith communities in this diverse and multicultural city. How do these Christian initiatives view people who believe different things than they do, and how do they structure themselves for engagement (if at all) for shared life with their multi-faith, affable-agnostic, or angry-atheist neighbour? With an awareness that the face of Christianity appears to be changing in Vancouver, reflecting less of the European immigrant culture from east of the Rocky Mountains and more of the Asian Christianity arriving through recent immigration (as well as historic pre-Confederation Asian heritage), how does that impact the way Christian initiatives organize themselves in this urban context and relate to the wider culture? As Bevans, Schroder, and Luzbetak argue, "we are now living in a 'world church' where most Christians are from the Majority World. David Barrett's statistical studies have basically confirmed this shift, and Philip Jenkins has predicted that by 2025 fully two-thirds of Christians will live in 'Africa, Latin America, and Asia … scholars are unanimous in acknowledging the accuracy of the facts. The 'average Christian' today is female, black, and lives in a Brazilian *favela* or an African village."[21] As Binney, Ngwa, and Barreto note, "the urbanized Christian not only hears the voices of fellow citizens in the city of current residence, but also the voices from sending cities (across nations and continents), and perhaps even the voices from traditional ancestral and rural settings which resurge in the larger urban centers in unanticipated ways."[22] Fieldwork will want to attend to the significant demographic changes, due to immigration, that are impacting Christianity in Vancouver.

As well, building on the work of many practical theologians such as Pete Ward, Christian Scharen, Natalie Wigg-Stevenson, and Christopher James, missiologist Scott Hagley's scholarship on a "missional sensibility to ethnography" will be especially important in the qualitative research ahead. Hagley argues that rather than a fixed identity or future telos, "the missional church is liberated for God's mission *by* and *through* the neighbor, the stranger, the other in and through the ministry of the Holy Spirit."[23] Therefore, while ethnographic theology tends to describe human experience of God as mediated through the practices and narratives of an ecclesial community, we must go further in our inquiry to discover a missional perspective.[24] This missional "sensibility" for fieldwork, according to Hagley, attends to the spaces and relationships where the "status quo of congregational life is challenged or provoked by new relationships or unexpected partnerships."[25] In other words, it is where the Christian initiative engages in deliberate "boundary crossing," where a rich understanding of missional engagement awaits. Hagley describes this missional sensibility in relationship to ethnography by noting that it, "*emerges from* and *attends to* boundary crossing movements of the congregation; ethnography becomes missional theology at the place of disruption and difference, at the intersection and interaction between congregation and community."[26]

How will those involved in Vancouver Christian initiatives describe their experiences of this boundary-crossing action? Perhaps it will be similar to recent research by Barna Group in the United States that found 99 per cent of Christians involved in common good community projects with non-Christians reported increased happiness, 96 per cent felt inspired as part of the group, and 91 per cent became closer to God as part of the wider community connection.[27] It is noteworthy to compare those findings to Barna Group's recent survey of American Protestant pastors where only 5 per cent ranked community engagement as their top priority and less than 50 per cent of their churches even collected information on the community needs outside their church.[28]

Missional Rhetoric vs Missional Practice

Missional theology emphasizes God's agency in the world and invites Christians to engage alongside God in repairing the world by seeing neighbours (and neighbourhoods) as subjects, rather than objects. Missional theology contends that "in mission, we encounter God in new and surprising ways, as God leads us in disruptive movements of the Spirit through our welcome of the stranger and announcement of the reign of God."[29] Will we find a correlation between this missional rhetoric and missional practice in the Christian initiatives visited in the fieldwork? Scott Hagley assists us in imaging what that missional practice might look like when he argues that there are "three habits necessary for missional discernment in relationship to congregational call: attending to surprise and disruption, risking theological speech, and facilitating experimental action."[30]

As we further develop our map of Vancouver, we will want to explore Christian initiatives' understanding of religious placemaking, noting the missional literature's emphasis upon incarnational expressions of presence in the neighbourhood. Are Christian communities living out their core convictions for the betterment of the community in which they gather? And what impact, if any, does an online digital presence contribute to that sense of religious placemaking? As Pete Ward argues, the meaning of community shifts and changes over time. Ward writes that "community has not died, but it has changed. People still want to be with each other, they still want to feel that they have significant relationships, and they still want to make a difference in other people's lives. In liquid modernity this desire is expressed through constant communication. One example of this is the use of cell phones, which make it possible for us to communicate with friends and relatives while we are on the move."[31] As Paul Fiddes argues, "we live in a world where space is less the confined space of established social groups, and more the open arenas of global networks of information and communication."[32] Here, Vancouver-based journalist Michael Harris's publications on the impact of technology on community are helpful in raising questions of what communities have potentially gained or lost through the digital revolution. In his Governor General's Award–winning book *The End of Absence*, Harris notes the importance of being a "digital immigrant" born before 1985, and knowing what life is like both with the Internet and without, so that one can be a "fluent translator of Before and After."[33]

DEVELOPING THE FIELD GUIDE

The four curiosities named in the preceding section help fuel the research on the ground as we attempt to create thick(er) descriptions of Christian witness in Vancouver. As we pack our bag for the journey ahead, we bring with us hypotheses to test:

1   There is a correlation between relational connection to neighbour and ability to share the gospel or "witness" to one outside the faith community. (witness and language)

2 The broader secular nature of Vancouver places pressure upon, and creates urgency in, the Christian community's need to form Christian identity in a more fulsome way. (theological identity and the secular context)

3 There is an ongoing question about soteriology in the Vancouver context, both within and outside the Christian community, as it is relates to the care for creation and widely shared environmental ethics as well as respect for Indigenous culture and spirituality. (theological identity and the secular context)

4 The significant impact of immigration on Vancouver, especially from Asia, appears to be changing the composition of Christian initiatives. This boundary crossing across cultures and socio-economic groups is an essential part of missional theology in praxis and is impacting both church and city. (witness and language, bridging and diversity, missional rhetoric vs missional practice)

5 While missional theology places a great emphasis upon the religious placemaking of the neighbourhood, the pre- and post-pandemic emphasis upon digital community is challenging the geographic or liminal space assumptions of what it means to be part of a "parish." (bridging and diversity, missional rhetoric vs missional practice)

Before starting on our journey, however, we attend further to the methodology employed through this qualitative fieldwork: we develop a field guide to lead us.[34] Unlike the fieldwork of other scholars in urban ethnographic and ecclesiastical studies focused on a particular congregation (e.g., Scott Hagley[35] or Natalie Wigg-Stevenson[36]) or a particular neighbourhood (e.g., Johannes Riphagen[37]), the fieldwork for Vancouver is more like Christopher James's city-wide focus in Seattle. As a result, the engagement of Christian initiatives in Vancouver in the next chapter is more of a "quick ethnographic"[38] study of a diverse group of faith communities than a deep dive on a particular congregation or agency. The language of "quick" or "rapid" ethnographic study is contested within academia, and it could be argued that these brief encounters between myself as the researcher and the leaders and the participants in the different initiatives might better be described as case studies. My choice to use "quick ethnographic study" comes from my work with Professor Miranda Klaver, cultural anthropologist at Vrije Universiteit Amsterdam, who uses this description for her work visiting sites for brief interviews and participant observation exercises.

As the researcher, my selection process for the field sites included initial conversation with a variety of initiative leaders (often perceived as "gatekeepers"), many of whom participated in the pastor focus group described below. I was seeking field sites that would provide a diverse sample across Vancouver neighbourhoods and a robust ecumenical sample. The method of studying these Christian initiatives involved a four-step process briefly described in chapter 1:

1 an exploration of the initiative's Internet presence (website, social media, blogs, and podcasts) for its explicit beliefs and practices
2 a walking conversation with the initiative leader (pastor or executive director) to better determine the social location, history, and ecological frame[39] of the Christian initiative[40]
3 a site visit (online gathering)[41] to the Christian initiative for their worship or other gathering for participant observation of the community's common life, practices, and other implicit actions
4 a focus group interview[42] on Zoom[43] in a synchronous, semi-structured format with three to five participants[44] from each initiative visited (in step 3) following a list of standard questions[45]

The focus group interviews in the various Christian initiatives all responded to the same list of questions developed, in part, in reference to the "sensitizing concepts"[46] and hypotheses identified earlier in this chapter.[47] Study of these focus groups attended primarily to idiographic knowledge through "knowledge of the other," while acknowledging the corresponding "knowledge of phenomena" and "reflexive knowing" that emerged.[48] These interview questions were framed to address the guiding question in this book: "How are Christians in Vancouver today, as a minority expression of the majority secular population, organizing their communities, shaping their beliefs, and expressing themselves in mission?"

Discerning the meaning that participants ascribe to various practices is a challenge; as Hans Schaeffer notes, "within ecclesial contexts, practices are likely to convey several layers of meaning that form a complex texture of traditioned presuppositions, contextual situatedness, and personal intentions."[49] Discernment is not limited to human agency and understanding, however, for while this fieldwork is a study of Christian initiatives and their missional interaction with the city of Vancouver, the research takes seriously Claire Watkin's claim that we are not concerned "simply with human practice, change and agency as such; but ... also ... our ultimate concern (is) with the discernment of God's agency within these human practices."⁵⁰ Darrell Guder concurs when he writes: "It is the particularity of God working out God's mission through a certain people that missional and practical theologies overlap ... These theological convictions center on God's action in gathering a people to witness to the healing of all creation."⁵¹

In order to attend to this divine agency and help discern the "motivating beliefs and spiritualities of Christian communities" in the "dusty corners" (to borrow David Bosch's language) of Vancouver's Christian communities, focus group conversations involved lay people from various Christian initiatives. Practically speaking, the lay participants in the focus group were invited by the leader of the initiative, with my encouragement to select as diverse a sample of their community as possible (age, gender, ethnicity, socio-economic). The focus groups attempted to hear the perspectives "from the pews" on questions of missional interaction with the city of Vancouver and the corresponding motivating beliefs and organizational forms of Christian community.⁵²

Noting this perceived gap in understanding between leadership and participants, the focus group conversations were studied for evidence of what Helen Cameron and colleagues call the Four Theological Voices Model, attending to the normative, formal, espoused, and operant theologies at work in their particular Christian initiative.⁵³ The four voices of theology is an approach that invites critique, however, with concern about how to differentiate between an individual's "espoused and operant theology" and that of the whole group. Clare Watkins acknowledges the limits of the four voices approach and notes the assumption that the voices belong closely to one another and are intrinsically interrelated, while noting that the operant voice is particularly difficult to identify since there is a "surdic" quality to lived reality that is challenging to account for.⁵⁴ Sarah Dunlop has suggested that visual ethnographic methods can support practical theologians investigating the "elusive operative voice within the four voices" as they seek to understand more fully the way people live out their faith convictions.⁵⁵ In using the four voices model, congregations are, in the words of Pete Ward, "embodied, communal theology" and can be "read" just like theological books; however, they differ from books in the sense that their theology is not necessarily coherent or systematic but, rather, a continuing dialogue or debate between different (and sometimes contradicting) voices.⁵⁶ Nevertheless, the four voices of theology remains a helpful tool to locate a particular Christian initiative within a larger Christian denominational tradition, while studying focus groups for how members understand the mission, theology, and organization of their initiative compared to the "official" narrative.

In building the interview guide[57] for the Zoom focus groups, the following questions were developed:

1 In your experience, describe what values or beliefs – whether or not they are Christian – Vancouverites have in common? (theological identity and the secular context)

2 What do you think the wider (ecumenical) church's mission should be across Vancouver and how does your local church (Christian initiative) participate in that mission? (missional rhetoric vs missional practice)

3 When you think back over the past five years, what is the most effective form of mission (best practice) that your church (Christian initiative) has used (performed) to reach people in Vancouver? (missional rhetoric vs missional practice)

4 What is the most significant difference (age, gender, ethnicity, socio-economic) between the people who are part of your church (Christian initiative) and those whom you encounter (outside of church) on a daily basis in your neighbourhood? (bridging and diversity)

5 Who are the partners in the wider community (faith-based or otherwise) that your church (Christian initiative) works with to achieve your mission? (bridging and diversity)

6 Tell me a story about a time that you discussed your Christian faith with someone in Vancouver (neighbour, co-worker, family, stranger) outside your local church (Christian initiative)? What happened and how did the other person respond? (witness and language)

7 What helps or hinders you when it comes to sharing your Christian beliefs with others (outside your faith community) in Vancouver? (witness and language)

8 Given Vancouverites' identified value for Indigenous culture, as well as its corresponding environmental values, how might Christians better engage this emphasis upon First Nations and creation for the sake of Christian mission in the city? (theological identity and the secular context)

Attending as well to research ethics, before each Zoom interview I explained the aims of the research, the nature of the interview, and an overview of what would be discussed. I asked for informed consent verbally to record the conversation and anonymized the interview data for the focus groups, with participants identified only by their Christian initiative. Following the distinction offered by Eileen Campbell-Reed and Christian Scharen between confidentiality and secrecy, participants were encouraged in the group interview to protect each other's confidence by not sharing the stories of other participants outside of the interview.[58] Participants were given a "Participant Consent Form," fieldnotes were kept, as well as Zoom recordings captured of each interview (videos deleted at the end of the research), and a review of the data involved a process of open, focused, and selective coding based on grounded theory qualitative data analysis.[59] These labels or codes helped structure my interpretation of the data and presentation of the fourteen Christian initiatives in the chapters to follow. In the engagement with local communities of Christian faith I echo Nancy Ammerman's observation that the study of congregations must be done with "great humility and care," noting that the object of study is "after all, a human community filled with people whose lives must be treated with respect."[60]

In the fieldwork, I attempted to balance a commitment to visiting Christian initiatives as a university-based researcher with a lens of observation and analysis with being reflexive and transparent as a Vancouver Christian professor and pastor bringing my own experience and perceptions to bear on the study of a site, some of which I had visited previously and even preached in their services. To that end, I was aware of my positionality in this work with my role as researcher, practical theologian, and "neutral observer," with the autoethnographic elements that challenge that perspective. Canadian anthropologists Lynda Mannik and Karen McGarry acknowledge the critique of autoethnography,[61] yet argue for its role in research in the Canadian context given a growing awareness of post-colonial lenses and Indigenous epistemologies. Mannik and McGarry argue that autoethnography "systematically analyzes the personal experiences and emotions of anthropologists to interrogate the methods and theories of the discipline while also adding dimension to the studies of others and others' cultures."[62] Additionally, while conducting fieldwork for this book, the variety of field notes kept included mental notes, jotted notes, and full field notes, as well as recording of the Zoom interviews.[63]

As noted in chapter 1, this fieldwork in qualitative research was undertaken as an act of practical theology defined by Swinton and Mowat as "critical, theological reflection on the practices of the Church as they interact with the practices of the world, with a view to ensuring and enabling faithful participation in the continuing mission of the triune God."[64] Through the research methods of conversation with leadership, website and social media research, and site visits and focus groups, the fieldwork attempted to follow best practices of credibility, transferability, dependability, and confirmability in qualitative research.[65] By analyzing the data produced, identifiable themes emerged in response to the research question, primarily through description and interpretation. The following chapters address possible proposals regarding what a thicker description of missional interactions with the city of Vancouver teaches us about the motivating beliefs and spiritualities of Christian communities. Five key themes emerged from the data while coding the fieldwork: space, building, and geography; Christian identity and Christian self-understanding; sexuality and cultural politics; witness and mission; and spirituality and social status.

By "space, building, and geography," I attend to the common themes that emerged regarding neighbourhood distinctives, ecclesiastical space (whether it was scarce or undergoing redevelopment), and the ways in which the initiative was connected to the neighbourhood. As Philip Sheldrake argues, "a sense of 'place' is one of the categories of human experience with the greatest impact on how we understand the world and situate ourselves in it."[66] "Christian identity and Christian self-understanding" emerged through site visits to worship services and conversations with pastors and focus groups that described their initiative's theological distinctives and how they related to the wider Vancouver context. "Sexuality and cultural politics" attends to the clear emphasis in many of the initiatives studied regarding their position on LGBTQ+ inclusion (or not), as well as how they addressed wider issues in Vancouver including Indigenous culture and the environment. "Witness and mission" identifies the specific ways in which an initiative understood its impact of Christian thought and practice on the wider Vancouver context. Finally, "spirituality and social status" attempts to name the ways in which Christians in these initiatives described the broader context of Vancouver, particularly the beliefs of their non-Christian neighbours and the material values they hold.

PREPARING FOR THE FIELDWORK

Convening a pastor focus group was my final step. I met with fifteen Vancouver pastors from a diverse background of different genders, ethnicities, denominations, and Christian initiatives of various kinds, including church plants, established congregations, multi-site churches, and para-church agencies. As well, the pastors represented ministries from different neighbourhoods across the city of Vancouver. We engaged in discussion on the Vancouver context and the various forms of theology, mission, and organizational culture of their respective initiatives.

Participants noted the challenge of secularity in Vancouver, the rapidly changing urban demographics (Asian ethnicity in particular), and the shared values of Vancouverites regarding Indigenous culture and the environment. Pastors were keen to talk about the impact of COVID-19 on their various ministries and to share their concern that the pandemic would further contribute to the decline being experienced in some congregations or ministries. Comparisons were often made to other parts of North America where they had served in ministry prior to coming to Vancouver, and how this West Coast city seemed to be the most challenging for active, deeply committed Christian practice and belief.[67] I concluded the afternoon with an invitation for the Christian initiatives represented in the room to participate further in the fieldwork, which formed the core of the engagement that follows in the next chapter.

3

Hitting the Road

Visiting an Eclectic Mix of Vancouver's Christian Communities

VANCOUVER CHRISTIAN INITIATIVES

Having established some of the unique aspects of Vancouver's West Coast culture, packed our bag for the journey, which included careful study of the map (methodology), we now set off walking the streets of Vancouver, sitting in coffee shops with pastors, sliding into a pew for Sunday worship, reviewing websites and social media, and listening to lay people in focus groups for further understanding of the ways in which Christians are gathering, organizing, and engaging in mission. The fourteen sites visited in this chapter represent church plants, mainline Protestant congregations, ethnic-specific churches, multi-site evangelical congregations, neighbourhood-focused Christian communities, Roman Catholic and Orthodox parishes, and para-church agencies. As we hit the road, you will sometimes notice subtle and significant differences between the two sites studied in each category, as well as in comparisons across categories. In the next chapter we reflect more fully on what this may mean for our research question, "How are Christians in Vancouver today, as a minority expression of the majority secular population, organizing their communities, shaping their beliefs, and expressing themselves in mission?"

As noted at the end of chapter 2, the fieldwork is presented here after significant reflection and coding, organizing each of the fourteen sites to be viewed through the lenses of space, building, and geography; Christian identity and Christian self-understanding; sexuality and cultural politics; witness and mission; and spirituality and social status in the city. As mentioned in chapter 1, this research builds on Christopher James's work in nearby Seattle and uses his four models

Table 3.1
Fourteen Christian initiatives participating in the Vancouver study, 2021–22

Type of Christian community		
Church plant	Artisan Church	St Peter's Fireside
Mainline Protestant congregation	Oakridge United Church	St Paul's Anglican Church
Multi-site evangelical congregation	Tenth Church–Kitsilano	Tapestry Church–Marpole
Ethnic-specific congregation	Vancouver Chinese Presbyterian Church (温哥华华人长老会)	Pacific Grace Mennonite Brethren Church (基督教頌恩堂)
Neighbourhood focused	First Christian Reformed Church	Kitsilano Christian Community
Catholic/Orthodox congregation	Cathedral of Our Lady of the Holy Rosary (Roman Catholic)	St Gregory the Illuminator Armenian Apostolic Church (Orthodox)
Para-church agency	Sanctuary Mental Health Ministries	Jacob's Well

of Christian community[1] to assess the fourteen Christian communities. The formal fieldnotes kept during research are nearly two hundred pages long, and thus what follows is a highly condensed and analytical expression of the journey through those communities. Nevertheless, you will gain insight into common challenges and particular responses to sharing Christian faith in Canada's third-largest city. Vancouver missiologist Alan Roxburgh encourages people to act as "detectives of divinity,"[2] paying close attention to what is said, observed, and valued in order to gain a better understanding of divine and human agency at work in Vancouver's churches today. As we set off, here is the road map for our adventure:

CHURCH PLANTS

Artisan Church

Artisan Church is a church plant founded in 2009 by the Mennonite Brethren tradition through their C2C Collective church planting network.[3] Artisan Church's vision, appearing on their website and quoted often by the pastor and focus group participants, is joining

Figure 3.1 The Japanese Hall in Vancouver's Downtown Eastside where Artisan Church meets

"God in the renewal of all things" in their lives and neighbourhood, echoing the Neighborhood Incarnation model of Christopher James's work.[4] The website describes the church's desire for people to not simply "attend church, but to be the church … creating an alternative culture that embodies Jesus' love in the city."[5] Reflecting the high cost of real estate in Vancouver, combined with a decreasing number of ecclesiastical buildings available for rent, Artisan Church now meets in the Japanese Hall in the Downtown Eastside neighbourhood, with offices a few blocks away in an old warehouse building.[6]

When I attended their worship gathering, the community was a mix of ages and ethnicities with a demographic that leaned towards young adults and young families. Pastor Nelson Boschman preached a forty-one-minute sermon[7] that included silence, reflection on a spiritual practice, and feedback from the congregation. Here Artisan Church echoes Scott Hagley's observations in his fieldwork at Midtown Church, with its emphasis upon practice that "invites improvisation and conversation" that include "shared meaningful activities" that "demands we continuously learn from others within the practice."[8] By integrating spiritual practice into the teaching time, Pastor Boschman offered worship participants an opportunity to experiment for themselves and share with others their experience of Christian practice.

Distinctive of Artisan Church is the eight-page statement published in January 2021 entitled "Milestone Statement on LGBTQ+ Inclusion," which explains their movement towards full inclusion and away from their official ties with the Mennonite Brethren denomination.[9] Pastor Boschman explained to me that several years into the church plant, conversation kept emerging around how the church would engage the LGBTQ+ community in Vancouver. The leadership team guided the congregation through a time of prayer, study, reflection, and discernment on the issue. The result was the Milestone document that described their arrival as a Christian community that would be an inclusive space for LGBTQ+ people and their allies.[10] Artisan offers a similar example to EastLake Community Church in Christopher James's study of Seattle that changed its position to "fully include LGBTQ persons in all areas of church life."[11] Highlighting how contested the issue of human sexuality is in Vancouver's ecclesiastical context, the Mennonite Brethren conference met in 2021 and asked Artisan Church to "repent" of their inclusion statement. When Artisan Church refused, the church plant was "released" from the denomination.[12] Pastor Boschman reflected on the tumult of that time and how pleased he was that most church members remained with Artisan Church, even after going through that difficult passage with the denomination.[13]

Now as an independent congregation, Artisan is placing an emphasis on its specific context stating, "we are committed to the unity of our sister churches in the Downtown Eastside of Vancouver. We collaborate in prayer, support and organize several joint functions/ gatherings each year."[14] Outreach ministries are coordinated with other existing ministries such as Jacob's Well, Compassion Canada, and the Mennonite Central Committee. Focus group participants noted, however, that Artisan Church's mission is "yet to be defined." "Some want to have a particular mission to the poor in the Downtown Eastside," observed one participant, "and yet the vast majority of our membership do not reside there or have connection other than a Sunday." Others noted that the mission of Artisan is to be "a broken wing church," as a place of healing and rest for those who have been hurt by other churches, "where people are holding on by a string and gather at Artisan to continue to practice our faith." One said that "an emphases on the arts and celebrating people as they are, rather than trying to change people, has become a key part of the mission of the church. Don't get me wrong, transformation and renewal happen at Artisan, but it is organic rather than programmatic." Here, Artisan Church reflects Christopher James's New Community model with a "distain for proselytism and evangelistic appeals."[15]

Both the pastor and focus group participants noted the difference between who attends Artisan Church and those who live in the neighbourhood. Artisan has a higher socio-economic and class status as well as a younger demographic than those around them in the community. As well, race was identified as a difference: "We're mostly a white congregation, although we're trying to increase the diversity of the congregation. For example, we meet only a few blocks from Chinatown, but that diversity is not well represented in our congregation." Reflecting on the wider values of Vancouverites in the city, Artisan members noted Vancouverite's love of nature, left-leaning political culture, and high value on material possessions that mark their status, from expensive sports cars to fashion clothing. One participant said, "even your gym membership sets you apart. It's a symbol for something. There is a sense that belonging to the more exclusive private gyms puts you on a higher social stratum." Participants also identified the ongoing struggle with belonging. "Vancouver is a hard place to meet people and that is in part because people value their privacy and individualism here."

St Peter's Fireside

St Peter's Fireside, a church plant founded by The Reverend Alastair Sterne in 2011 as part of the Anglican Network in Canada, is located in the downtown core of Vancouver. The website has a crisp and inviting look with images of Vancouver, as well as imagery yoked to the church's key biblical verse: John 21.[16] The vision of St Peter's Fireside is described this way: "Our vision is simple: Jesus is alive and renewing everything – our city, its people, even us – and we get to be part it!"[17]

The church plant rents space on Sunday mornings in the University of British Columbia's extension campus known as Robson Square, beneath the Vancouver Art Gallery.[18] The space itself feeling a little cavernous, a traditional university lecture hall that the leadership even referred to as a "bunker." Like Artisan Church, the average age of a worship participant was in their twenties or thirties, of a higher socioeconomic status. The focus group described the identity of the church

Figure 3.2 UBC Robson Square where St Peter's Fireside rents space

plant as joining God in the renewal of Vancouver through translating
the gospel in a way that downtown professionals can understand. One
participant said, "I have no trouble recommending or inviting people
to St Peter's Fireside. I know people will come and not have a weird
experience. They will get a good service and sermon and not be turned
off the faith." The participant paused and then said, "I invite people
who are 'Christian-adjacent,' open to the church, without worrying
that they will think I'm weird for going to church." Sarah Wilkins-
Laflamme has identified the "Christian-adjacent" friends of the
"religious millennial"[19] in the focus group as a "cultural believer
millennial," who has a high probability of religious affiliation and
belief in God in their own way but a relatively low average frequency
of religious behaviours, or a "spiritual seeker millennial," who has a
high probability of religious affiliation and who believes in God in
their way but exhibits a willingness to experience spiritual practice
both in and outside of institutional religion.[20]
    While there are "hints" of the Anglican connection to St Peter's
Fireside, one must dig into the website to identify the specific connection to the Anglican Network in Canada, a movement that left the

Anglican Church of Canada in opposition to its growing LGBTQ+ inclusion.[21] Even with subtle elements of Anglican liturgy throughout the service, the overall experience fits what Killen and Mark identify in their Pacific Northwest fieldwork as "sectarian entrepreneur," including a "world-affirming worship style" that includes "a critique of the world but certainly not an outright rejection of contemporary forms of communication or the media" and a "message … that the Christian religion gives one remarkable rewards if one commits to its exclusivist theology."[22] Indeed, even the location of St Peter's Fireside offers evidence of what Stefan Paas has identified as "sectarian church planting," embodying distinctive doctrinal or ecclesiological convictions with the church plant located across the street from Christ Church Cathedral, which is part of the more liberal Anglican Church of Canada.[23] In worship and conversation with participants, "counter-witness" emerged as a key principle of engagement with the city. Here, the initiative echoes Michael Wilkinson's study of evangelicals in Cascadia who do not assume they are serving a nominally Christian society, and instead view themselves as missionaries in a cultural context that is unlike their own subculture and in need of transformation.[24] The focus group remarked on how Christians in Vancouver offer a different way of thinking, being, and living from their secular neighbour. One participant said that "the kingdom of God is visible in the culture and nature, but God reveals himself in concrete ways in Christian community. The churches in Vancouver should embody that vision in a loving and non-judgmental way." St Peter's Fireside primarily reflected elements of James's Great Commission Team approach with both a drive to reach others evangelistically and a sense of obligation to do so.[25]

Another participant noted how the response from Vancouverites to Christianity depended on whether they had any kind of background with faith. "There are two kinds of people in Vancouver you bump into. The first are de-churched. They have some vague memory, and they'll talk a bit once they find out you're a Christian, and usually tell you why they don't go anymore. Then there are the secular people with zero background. They're harder to connect with. They'll hear that you're a Christian and just not be at all interested in talking about spiritual things. They just want to change the topic."

Participants were all in agreement that the most significant thing that helps in sharing Christian faith is pre-existing relationships with other people. They noted that in Vancouver it is difficult to engage in

a sustained faith conversation with another person if there is no pre-
existing and positive relationship – whether it be a friend, family
member, or co-worker. One participant said, "it's important too when
engaging others, you know, to just keep faith talk casual and not
make a big deal out of it. I tell people, 'Yeah, I go to church on
Sunday. It's great. you should come with me.'" Focus group participants noted that Vancouverites have a common commitment to care
for the environment, respect individuality, and maintain politeness
with others. They also named a fourth value as "status." The group
discussion noted that Vancouverites value where they eat out, the
clothes they wear, and the cars they drive. One participant said, "at
a party people talk about real estate, nature, where you eat out, where
your kids go to school, the car you drive, and how people have an
expectation that institutions and authorities are there to meet our
needs." What was clear in the focus group conversations is that there
was a shared value in inviting non-Christians to worship and a sense
that the church plant was a space where people could encounter
Christianity as a transformative space. This raises the question of
whether church plants are more likely to see conversion growth rather
than transfer growth. While many scholars contest the claim that
church plants "make more converts," Richard Pitt believes it to be
true in his study of 135 church plants in America, arguing, "it also
seems that planted churches have an easier time than established
churches reaching those who are not currently involved in the church.
This isn't to say that established churches can't reach them, but that
other concerns take precedence, like caring for the population they
already have. Older churches naturally reallocate resources toward
maintaining their current membership and constituents, instead of
those outside their walls. New churches, however, have no choice but
to focus on non-members to get their venture off the ground. Some
of the new leaders may recently have come from the unchurched,
making them more sensitive to this group. Additionally, if the
unchurched have different desires for what they want in a church, a
new church may be able to meet these more easily because they can
tailor the church to these desires."[26] Both church plants in the study
placed a great emphasis on welcoming either those hurt by religion
(Artisan Church) or those with no religious background (St Peter's
Fireside) living in Vancouver's downtown core. Will that same commitment to welcome and discipleship be present in the other sites
visited in this study?

Figure 3.3 Oakridge United Church's new building

MAINLINE PROTESTANT CONGREGATIONS

Oakridge United Church

Oakridge United Church is described on the website as "the historic church on the corner of 41st Avenue and Elizabeth in the Oakridge neighbourhood" that underwent redevelopment with "a new building that opened in 2020."[27] Oakridge United Church's new facility on West 41st Avenue is a short walk from the Canada Line Skytrain station at Oakridge Centre. The neighbourhood is undergoing massive change with the CA$5-billion Oakridge Centre Mall project, including new stores and multiple high-rise condominium towers, being redeveloped as part of the City of Vancouver's Cambie Corridor and Oakridge Municipal Town Centre plan.[28] Oakridge United Church's story reflects the changing nature of ecclesiastical space in the city, where dwindling congregations are redeveloping to maintain a visible presence.[29] The Reverend Heather Joy James acknowledged both the opportunity and the challenge this new congregational facility presents with a modern, highly visible gathering space and significant financial support in the bank through the transaction with the developer.[30]

The desire for maintaining ecclesiastical space in the city as a witness was clear. Rev. Joy James showed me a backlit stained-glass window facing the alleyway that depicts a post-Resurrection Jesus Christ with the inscription, "He arose." "It's funny," Rev. Joy James said, "we don't even have a sign for the church on this back entrance, but this stained-glass window is an important witness to the world behind the church building." Philip Sheldrake would concur, arguing that "religious architecture is a bearer of specific ideas and symbols ... and understanding of human existence."[31] From Oakridge's online presence to site visits and conversations, the congregation's posture to the wider community included statements of welcome, hospitality, and inclusion. A focus group participant said: "Our most effective mission is displaying ways that show that we are inclusive. For example, we have a rainbow pride flag in our window. That's a powerful statement of our mission in the neighbourhood. We also show the pride flag digitally on the website and social media." Another participant stated that "there are more trans or gender-fluid people in the neighbourhood compared to the church. The church is more heterosexual in its makeup, but we're trying to change that." Like other congregations in this study, Oakridge also included a land acknowledgment on its website: "We are gathered on the traditional territory of the Musqueam, Tsleil-Waututh, and Squamish First Nations and gratefully acknowledge their stewardship of this land throughout the ages."

Rev. Joy James described the desire to begin outreach activities in their new building to engage neighbours, including a return to the Alpha course – a program designed to introduce people to Christianity – and, as a yoga instructor, offering Holy Yoga. There are also plans to use the coffee hour space as a weekday Christian café. Focus group participants also identified a connection with justice concerns, with one saying that "the church's mission is recognizing that Vancouverites are responsible for the environment and as Christians we come alongside neighbours as 'shepherds for the earth,' that's the church's role." Another participant said that "social justice is the wider church's mission in Vancouver by helping to address wrongs on a societal level and advocating for others." When reflecting on the specific mission of Oakridge United Church, participants said that "Oakridge helps people feel special. We provide a place for people to come and belong. Social justice is important as our mission." It was agreed that Oakridge United Church's mission includes a strong mission of hospitality. Here Oakridge demonstrated many of the features Christopher James's identifies in the New Community model, including hospitality and tolerance.[32] Connecting with neighbours was difficult, however, as one participant remarked: "The majority of the congregation is white, but the neighbourhood is primarily Asian." Another participant agreed, saying, "Yes, inside the church it is mostly kind elderly, Caucasian ladies, while outside in the neighbourhood it a mixed demographic and very much multinational." Sharing their Christian faith with others was difficult; as one participant said: "In general, when I've mentioned about going to church to others in Vancouver, people say things like, 'Oh, I used to go to church,' but I've never engaged in the question of why they don't go to church anymore."[33] As a congregation in the United Church of Canada, known as a more liberal Protestant denomination, conversations in the focus group reflected viewpoints that Matthew Hedstrom describes in his congregational studies as "religious cosmopolitanism," where there is "a greater awareness of the possibility that religious truth is multiple and that many forms of religious life and practice and identity may be individually and socially salubrious."[34] For example, in the focus group there were several comments about how the church did not "have all the truth" and that there were many "paths to enlightenment." James Wellman Jr and Katie Corcoran have identified the particular challenge for liberal Protestant churches in Cascadia as "naturally feel[ing] at home in the surrounding society" with its liberal values also having to work hard to "differentiate themselves from it," leading the researchers to conclude that "liberal Protestantism may be the toughest sell in the generally secular and liberal region."[35]

St Paul's Anglican Church

St Paul's Anglican Church is a historic parish of the Anglican Church of Canada in the Diocese of New Westminster located in the West End neighbourhood of downtown Vancouver. The church describes itself as being "in a season of change and renewal and we hope that people will feel called to join or partner with us, so that we become as diverse as the West End and Yaletown."[36] St Paul's Church dates back to 1889, three years after Vancouver was founded. St Paul's West End parish is one of the largest LGBTQI neighbourhoods in Canada. The sanctuary has the feel of a parish country church from rural England, while

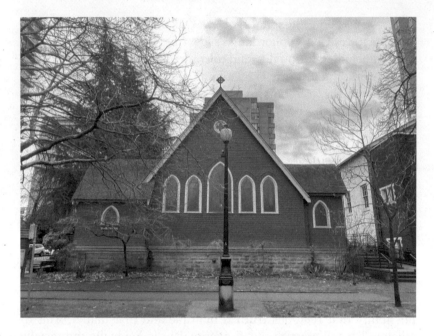

Figure 3.4 Historic St Paul's Anglican Church in the West End

the parish hall has a large labyrinth on the floor for people to engage in meditative practice. Walking with Reverend Philip Cochrane through the West End neighbourhood, he pointed out massive new condo towers a block from the church with the ubiquitous hipster coffee shops at street level. From the site visit for Sunday worship and subsequent conversations, their Christian identity is "progressive Anglican" with a particular focus on leading LGBTQ+ inclusion within the wider Anglican Church.[37]

Rev. Cochrane, as a LGBTQ+ person, reflected on the differences he experienced serving in the Church of England and now the Anglican Church of Canada, noting a narrower bandwidth of theological positions in Canadian Anglicanism. Reflecting on the polarization of the church on issues of human sexuality, Rev. Cochrane seemed restless to break through the traditional "liberal and conservative" divide. He spoke about the challenge of having St Paul's labelled as "the gay church," and how, even as a LGBTQ+ person, he hoped to develop the ministry team with people who represented a wider part of the community, including women and people of colour. His comments echo congregational studies like that of St Matthew's Church in Long

Beach, California, where LGBTQI members worked against being labelled and did not want to be a separate "gay church" where one member said, "we are part of the body of Christ, we are not the gay body of Christ. It doesn't matter what happens on this earth, I know that I'm a part of Christ. And I'm grateful."[38] Rev. Cochrane's resistance to labelling is similar to what Christopher James observed at New Community churches such as All Pilgrims that rejected "its designation by outsiders as a 'gay church' despite the fact that a strong majority of its members are part of the LGBTQ community."[39]

Focus group participants from St Paul's described residents in their West End neighbourhood as valuing community and belonging. This engagement took place daily with people frequenting local coffee shops and restaurants, strolling the beach at English Bay, and getting together with family and friends. Diversity was a shared value with their neighbours, with people of different ethnic backgrounds, sexual orientations, and religious beliefs residing in the West End. Individuality was a strong shared value for those in the neighbourhood as well as a common value placed on the natural surroundings and a love of the outdoors.

MULTI-SITE EVANGELICAL CONGREGATIONS

Tenth Church–Kitsilano (Tenth Kits)

Tenth Church, a multi-site congregation with locations across Vancouver, was founded by the Christian and Missionary Alliance denomination in 1935,[40] with a revival of the congregation beginning in the 1990s upon the arrival of former Sony executive Ken Shigematsu as pastor.[41] The commonly held vision is described as: "We are a place where people of all different backgrounds can discover Christ, a community of spiritual transformation that seeks social justice for all."[42]

Tenth Kits is pastored by Dan Matheson and serves the Kitsilano neighbourhood of Vancouver where young twenty-something singles or couples mostly live, close to popular "Kits beach," English Bay, and Stanley Park. It is an area full of small older apartments, trendy shops, and eclectic restaurants. Kitsilano is an expensive neighbourhood, and as we walked along Pastor Matheson noted how difficult it is to find a space to meet as a church plant. I asked him about the history of where Tenth Kits church has met. The congregation has

Figure 3.5 Tenth Church–Kitsilano meets at the Museum of Vancouver

rented several spaces over the years in Kitsilano, from a high school to a former Anglican Church of Canada building. At the time of our conversation Tenth was meeting at the Museum of Vancouver but were planning on moving again if they could find more suitable space. Following the conclusion of this research, Tenth Kits found space in Kerrisdale Presbyterian Church and moved their worship gatherings to the West Side neighbourhood of Vancouver. Tenth Kits reflected many of the characteristics of James's Neighborhood Incarnation model, but the challenge of Vancouver is how to be "in, of and for their neighborhood"[43] when it is so difficult to find permanent meeting space – ecclesiastical or otherwise.

In both site visits and conversation, it became clear that the "brand" of Tenth was important and a campus like Tenth Kits was closely connected with the larger identity of the multi-site congregations. I asked Pastor Matheson what the advantages were of being part of a wider multi-site congregation, including the support he received during the stress and strain of the COVID-19 pandemic. He spoke highly of the leadership of Ken Shigematsu as senior pastor of the main Mount Pleasant site. The collegiality of the campus pastors meeting together is a great strength to him. I asked how much freedom he had to make his own decisions as part of a multi-site congregation.[44] Matheson laughed when he described their shared leadership philosophy as "chaordic" – a mash-up of chaos and order. This chaordic approach to the multi-site church works, according to Pastor Matheson, due to a shared vision for ministry in the city honouring Jesus, good communication between site pastors, and a kind of holy restlessness to keep reaching for ways to connect with Vancouverites who do not yet know Jesus.[45]

Tapestry Church–Marpole

Tapestry Church is one church with four congregations "woven together in faith"; the main campus is in Richmond, a suburb of Vancouver. Unlike Tenth Church–Kitsilano, the other multi-site congregation in this study, Tapestry Church–Marpole has its own website that links to the main Tapestry Church in Richmond.[46] Tapestry Church, led by founding pastor Reverend Albert Chu, is part of the Christian Reformed denomination; Jesse Pals is the Marpole site pastor.

Marpole is a historic neighbourhood of south Vancouver, and Tapestry–Marpole began by renting space in a new high-rise building adjacent to the Canada Line subway station built for the 2010 Winter Olympics. The building included condos, retail outlets, restaurants, and a large Cineplex Odeon movie theatre, where the church met on Sunday mornings.[47] When the pandemic started, everything moved online, and Tapestry–Marpole cancelled their month-by-month rental agreement for the movie theatre. Pastor Pals noted that while that site, as a new facility with great accessibility to transit, was initially helpful, it did not reflect the rest of the Marpole neighbourhood of low-rise apartment buildings and mixed-income families. The movie theatre "was bright and shiny, but that sometimes rubs off in unhelpful ways," he said. According to Pastor Pals, Marpole is a diverse neighbourhood with the "majority (visible) minority being Asian." There are many families in the neighbourhood renting a floor of an old house or a suite in one of the many low-rise apartments.

Mid-pandemic, Pastor Pals started looking for a new location to meet in a hybrid model (in person and online) and selected a space a few blocks away from the former movie theatre site at the Scottish

Figure 3.6 Tapestry Church–Marpole worshipping in the Scottish Cultural Centre

Cultural Centre. The older building, frequently rented for wedding receptions and dance lessons, was rooted in the community and had a more authentic and homier feel. Pastor Pals remarked that the move caused little disruption to their church community, noting that there is always "a core and a crowd" in a church.[48]

Pastor Pals described walking the streets of Marpole over the years, praying for the neighbourhood, meeting neighbours, and building partnerships. He encourages members of Tapestry–Marpole to invest in mission and build relationships in "the six square blocks in one of Vancouver's oldest villages." Pastor Pals suggested that the role of church members was to "inhabit the neighbourhood" and to be on mission wherever God sent them that week – at work or home. Pastor Pals lamented that the pandemic abruptly ended a growing ministry with a nearby affordable housing project: members of Tapestry–Marpole would go two nights a month to cook a meal with residents and share conversation or watch the hockey game on television together. Here, Tapestry–Marpole reflects James's Neighborhood Incarnation model where they engage in boundary crossing and "actively seek to connect with persons across the socio-economic, generational, and cultural barriers that are present within their neighborhoods."[49]

ETHNIC-SPECIFIC CONGREGATIONS

Vancouver Chinese Presbyterian Church
(温哥华华人长老会)

The Vancouver Chinese Presbyterian Church was founded in 1895 in downtown's Chinatown neighbourhood and moved several decades ago to its current location on Cambie Street in Oakridge. At the time of this research, the congregation was completing a new building, replacing the 1980 structure with a new worship and meeting space, combined with twenty market-rate residential rental units, sixty-eight child-care spaces, fifty-six vehicle parking spaces, and – in a growing Vancouver trend – thirty-one bicycle spaces.

When asked what the most significant difference was between those who gathered at Vancouver Chinese Presbyterian Church and the surrounding Oakridge neighbourhood, focus group participants named several things. First, most members commute to the congregation and do not live in the immediate neighbourhood. Second, the neighbourhood is changing, ever since the Canada Line subway was built on the Cambie Corridor for the 2010 Winter Olympics. That development brought tremendous growth in high-rise condos. "I'm not sure we really know who our neighbour is anymore around here," said one participant. Third, it was recognized that there was a large Mandarin-speaking community in the neighbourhood, almost all recent wealthy immigrants from China. The challenge with reaching this community, noted one participant, was that most members in the church spoke Cantonese not Mandarin. Fourth, the congregation itself was mixed, with the Chinese-language services attended by older, lower-income (on pension) members, some of whom still live in Vancouver's historic Chinatown, and the English-language services attended by younger, more highly educated, higher-income members whose greater mobility enables commuting from different Vancouver neighbourhoods. Finally, it was noted that the number of young adults had been decreasing over the last several years so that now, even in the English-language ministry, 80 per cent are sixty years of age or older. That's a much older demographic in the church than those who live in the neighbourhood.

The Reverend Morgan Wong shared with me how the identity of the church reflects the different waves of immigration from Asia. The original community experienced discrimination, including lower wages

Figure 3.7 New Vancouver Chinese Presbyterian Church building

compared to Vancouverites from European backgrounds, as well as
overt racism, including the Chinese Head Tax that continued into the
late 1940s. The next wave was university students, mostly Cantonese-
speaking, in the 1950s through the 1970s. Before the handover of
Hong Kong from Britain to China in the 1990s, Cantonese-speaking
immigration to Vancouver significantly increased and those who came
did so with wealth to invest. The subsequent wave in the late 1990s
and into the early 2000s saw the profile of immigrants change yet
again, with wealthy individuals and families moving from mainland
China and being almost entirely Mandarin-speaking. Pastor Wong
noted how each of these waves had their own distinctives in culture,
identity, and need, thus pressing the Chinese Presbyterian Church
to try to adapt as needed for the sake of mission. This is especially
true when it comes to offering ministry to those in the 1.0, 1.5, or
2.0 generations. As a result, Pastor Wong mentioned how often the
children of those who grow up in the church end up going to other
churches as they leave home. "They're not rebelling but simply finding
their way in life, just as they've left their parent's house, so they leave
the church for another."

The congregation's mission appeared to be focused on connecting with the Chinese community through the existing ministries of the church listed on the website under "outreach," including a prayer wall, welcome ministry, communion ministry, hospitality ministry, scripture ministry, children's ministry, and music ministry.

Pacific Grace Mennonite Brethren Church
(基督教頌恩堂)

Pacific Grace Mennonite Brethren began in 1963, worshipping in both English and German, with "a few ethnic Chinese participating." By 1977, 80 per cent of the congregation were Chinese in ethnicity, and they dissolved the English-language ministry, leaving only a Chinese-language worship service. The congregation experienced numeric growth. Instead of looking for a larger building, they planted other congregations, including Burnaby Pacific Grace Chinese Church in 1990, Vancouver Pacific Grace Chinese Church in 1995, and North Shore Pacific Grace MB Church in 1997. An English-language ministry was reintroduced in the church and some from that ministry helped plant South Hill Church in 2007, a multi-ethnic congregation. In 1998, the "Chinese" label was dropped from the title, the congregation naming itself "Pacific Grace Mennonite Brethren Church." In 2009, the former Renfrew United Church closed, and Pacific Grace MB Church purchased the building. They currently worship in this highly visible location on East 1st Avenue, a neighbourhood of low-rise retail buildings with small single-detached homes.

Pacific Grace MB Church has three distinct ministries – the original Cantonese-language service with about forty-five regular members, a smaller Mandarin-language service with about twenty members, and the English-language ministry with about seventy-five members.[50] It was noted by the focus group that the neighbourhood is overwhelmingly Asian in its makeup, and in that sense the congregation reflects the neighbourhood. When they discussed the topic further, one difference noted was in socio-economic status. Overall, the members of the congregation were seen to be at a higher economic and educational level (many young professionals) than the general population around the church. It was observed that in their former building in the Hastings and Venables neighbourhood of Vancouver, the socio-economic gap was much larger than in their new East Vancouver neighbourhood. Back then, there were no church members living in

Figure 3.8 Signboard outside Pacific Grace Mennonite Brethren Church in East Vancouver

the neighbourhood. Today, there are many who walk to Pacific Grace Church services.

The posture towards the world outside the church was one that mirrored what Christopher James describes in Seattle as Great Commission Team churches that are highly conscious of the urban, progressive values around them while describing "their context as an urgent and strategic mission field."[51] The focus group offered good examples of how engagement with the wider city, including Indigenous people, refugee support, or neighbourhood children's programs, was clearly yoked to a strong desire to share the gospel and invite others into "the fellowship."

Pastor Bill Chan expressed his gratitude for the ministry he leads and placed his emphasis on making disciples for Jesus no matter where people ended up or what denomination they eventually called home. He observed the familiar pattern of some within the English-language ministry of Chinese churches who grew up in a church like Pacific Grace but then sought a less ethnically specific, pan-Asian expression of Christianity, such as Tenth Church or Tapestry, when they left home and married. Chan also noted the "Christian bubble" that many of his youth represented, kept within their specific Chinese community and almost all attending private Christian school. He commented on how the youth often struggled with understanding their more secular neighbours who do not hold to a Christian worldview. Chan identified his attempts to broaden his young members' understanding of the world around them in order to prepare for life beyond a private Christian education and ethnic-based church. He noted that too often the youth move into university and the wider world and simply fall away from the church. Of course, this falling away could be more in practice than in belief. Sam Hardy and Gregory Longo's research into declining adolescence religious behaviour suggests a distinction between "involvement but not importance ... thus, it seems that substantial decreases in religiousness are more normative across adolescence in terms of behavioural dimension (typically operationalized as religious worship service attendance) than the affective dimension (typically operationalized as religious importance)."[52]

Attending to that wider world, focus group participants described what hindered their Christian witness in Vancouver, naming the challenge of people's indifference or hostility to Christianity as well as the challenge of being engaged in faith conversations and not knowing how to answer difficult questions people ask about faith. "I prefer to bring people into a Christian fellowship small group, rather than try to answer people's difficult questions about faith," said one participant. Focus group members identified that the current political environment and culture in Canada makes it difficult to talk publicly about faith. "Diversity is valued to the extreme in Vancouver, so that any particular faith is not welcome. When I try to share my faith, I find that people are not open to hearing about doctrine or theology."

NEIGHBOURHOOD FOCUSED

First Christian Reformed Church

First Christian Reformed Church is a congregation located in the neighbourhood of East Vancouver on Victoria Drive. The church's purpose and mission are described as: "Our goal is that those of all ages and backgrounds will encounter God's love in worship and community times to be inspired to live out our faith in the rhythms of our lives."[53] The congregation articulates this vision for their community

Figure 3.9 First Christian Reformed Church with Immigrant Services Society
of British Columbia headquarters located next door

as: "From our youngest in children's ministries to those in their later
years, we share rhythms of eating, gardening, and celebrating together,
learning from, caring for and supporting each other, and pursuing
justice and advocacy with refugees together."[54]

First Christian Reformed Church is in the east Vancouver neighbourhood of Kensington-Cedar Cottage across the street from a large
modern building – the headquarters of a non-profit organization called
the Immigrant Services Society of British Columbia." The impressive
structure was built five years ago and offers day services for refugees
as well as eighteen temporary housing units.[55]

The posture of the congregation is one of openness and inclusion
to those from different backgrounds and worldviews. The relational
connection to the Immigrant Services Society of British Columbia
meant that in conversations with both the pastor and the focus group,
there was a great openness to receive and engage those of different
views. While there is not an overt statement of inclusion in the congregation, there was evidence of inclusion in many forms, including
ethnic and socio-economic, and with Indigenous people. Human

sexuality was not specifically named despite the congregation's high value on inclusion in other areas.

Pastor Trevor Vanderveen commented in our conversation on the challenge of Christian witness in the heart of Vancouver. He told a story of how they started an Alpha course years ago as an introduction to the Christian faith but found that even the basic Christian content was beyond most of the residents in their neighbourhood. Instead, they continued with the community meal that preceded the course. Over time, people were drawn into the preparation, serving, and cleanup of the meal. Some of the meal participants eventually joined the Sunday morning community, but others said that they would not feel comfortable coming to a church service but did feel at home at the community meal.

This sense of hospitality as mission came through in the focus group too. As one participant remarked, "it's not just hospitality for the poor or at-risk street population, however. Hospitality goes further because Vancouver is so lonely and expensive. The church needs to build community where it is lacking." Another person noted that what the churches across Vancouver had in common, no matter what the denomination, was the call of Jeremiah 29 to "pray for the prosperity of the city and engage in God's reconciliation work for the healing of the nations. Trying to figure out what it means to love this city is important." Hospitality, inclusion, and deep relational connections in the neighbourhood offer evidence that First Reformed Church is closest to James's Neighborhood Incarnation model.[56]

Others commented on how the congregation's community garden has been a helpful connection place for church members, refugees living next door, and the wider neighbourhood. "With our basketball hoops in the yard, people gather," reflected one participant, "and refugees who come from a rural place love to wander through the community garden, helping to tend it and seeking friendship together with those who work there." Another recalled sitting in the community garden and greeting new neighbours who were inspecting the space from next door at the refugee welcome centre. "One little boy about seven years old was a Syrian refugee who didn't speak a word of English. He got all excited when he identified a garlic in the garden. It was something familiar and he taught me how to say garlic in his own language." Often, as Deanna Womack points out in her study of interfaith engagement in Christian congregations, "interreligious neighborliness [is] a task for the few rather than a calling for all of

Christ's followers" with leaders of interfaith movements viewing "mission and evangelism as detrimental to peaceful co-existence" or others with a "zeal for conversion [that] brings others to treat non-Christians as rivals and enemies."[57] Yet, leaders and lay people at First Christian Reformed Church consistently described their Christian mission to interfaith refugee neighbours in clear and inclusive ways that illustrated what Womack called "incarnational human relations" that provide the opportunity for mutual transformation.

Kitsilano Christian Community

Kitsilano Christian Community worships in the Fairview Baptist Church building in the Fairview neighbourhood of Vancouver that borders the area known as Kitsilano.[58] Pastor Monica McKinlay described the origin story of the congregation as a church plant three decades ago out of First Baptist Church in the downtown core of Vancouver, designed for those in the Kitsilano neighbourhood who were not traditionally connected with Christianity. For many years, the congregation met in rented space throughout Kitsilano, the longest rental location being in a public-school gymnasium. Pastor McKinlay became the minister three years ago, and they were already worshipping at Fairview Baptist Church building at that point.[59] The congregation's mission statement is, "we are a community rooted in Christ, growing together, bearing fruit in the world," and it describes itself as "a smallish church (one hundred people on an average Sunday) with a community feel, located on the edges of Kitsilano, Fairview, and Shaughnessy neighbourhoods in Vancouver." Affiliated with the Canadian Baptists of Western Canada, the congregation identifies and partners with mission projects in the community, which include the following. HomeStart Foundation, a local non-profit Christian humanitarian organization, helps people re-establish a home, including providing donated home furnishings to those in need. Kits Cares Café offers weekly café-style community meals at the Kitsilano Neighbourhood House in seeking to connect with those who are socially isolated or have physical needs. Kinbrace Refugee Housing and Support provides supportive transitional housing for refugee claimants in Vancouver.

Having been a church plant to Kitsilano, but no longer located in that neighbourhood, Pastor McKinlay describes her time with the congregation as one of "liminal space and community discernment,"

Figure 3.10 Fairview Baptist Church building where Kitsilano Christian Community gathers

seeking God's direction on how best they are to serve the neighbour-hood. She noted how the original birth narrative of the church plant decades ago was still at work in the congregation. "There's a loyalty to the Kitsilano neighbourhood, even when people don't live there anymore." But what if God was calling them to something new, she asked. Pastor McKinlay reflected that most of the members were keen to engage neighbours – however, not in traditional evangelistic models but rather more in shared life together to discern God's presence.

A significant identity marker for the congregation is its "Welcome Statement for LGBTQ2S+ friends" that quotes Romans 15:7: "Welcome one another, therefore, just as Christ has welcomed you for the glory of God." The congregation acknowledges that their Baptist denomination does not recognize same-sex marriage and there are "also some restrictions on LGBTQ2S+ Christians seeking ordination." However, as the welcoming statement notes, "beyond these areas, Baptist polity gives wide autonomy to local churches." The Welcoming Statement then declares: "We at Kitsilano Christian Community strongly believe that our primary call is to welcome everyone as they are, to treat all with love and respect, and give space for all to belong. Therefore, we at KCC want to explicitly welcome all LGBTQ2S+ Christians as full members. That is to say, any lay leadership position or lay ministry role at KCC is open to LGBTQ2S+ Christians. Furthermore, any LGBTQ2S+ person seeking Christ is welcome to fully participate and belong in the life and community of KCC." In conversation with Pastor McKinlay, we discussed the congregation's recent conversation that led to this "Welcome Statement for LGBTQ2S+ friends." Pastor McKinlay noted that as the wider denomination engaged in a discussion of human sexuality, same-sex marriage, and ordination of LGBTQ2S+ peoples, each congregation was encouraged to engage in conversation on the subjects. When Pastor McKinlay asked her leadership team about the possibility of a conversation, she found that there was unanimous approval both to engage in a discussion and to move towards a more public inclusive stand on human sexuality as a congregation. While the LGBTQ2S+ presence in the congregation is not large, McKinlay noted that within the wider Vancouver culture where her church members live, work, and play, acceptance of sexual diversity is now a given. The church reflected many of the characteristics of James's New Community model, including an "overly positive view" of progressive culture and a desire to engage the wider world in an inclusive welcome.[60] The relational connection with LGBTQ2S+ peoples in church members' own families was an additional factor, according to McKinlay. The conversation began before COVID-19, moved online during the pandemic, and in early 2021, the Welcoming Statement was adopted. I asked Pastor McKinlay what that meant for the congregation within the wider denominational system. She smiled and said, "Well, we were all encouraged to talk about the issue, but I imagine some will think we've gone too far." The congregation's overt inclusiveness towards

LGBTQ2S+ within a more conservative Baptist denomination bears hallmarks of what Lois Barrett and her colleagues identified in congregational studies as a missional pattern of "Taking Risks as a Contrast Community," whereby a missional church is "raising questions, often threatening ones" and "is grappling with ethical and structural implications of its missional vocation. It is learning to deal with internal and external resistance."[61] Kitsilano Christian Community and Artisan Church's pro-inclusion decisions, along with the lack of anti-inclusion language in the other non-mainline initiatives in the study is notable compared to Christopher James's study where LGBTQI inclusion was primarily amongst mainline church plants.[62]

CATHOLIC/ORTHODOX CONGREGATIONS

Cathedral of Our Lady of the Holy Rosary (Roman Catholic)

The Roman Catholic Cathedral of Our Lady of the Holy Rosary traces its roots back to 1885 when the Right Reverend Louis d'Herbomez, OMI, Vicar Apostolic of British Columbia, appointed Father Patrick Fay to care for the two settlements of Granville: Gastown and Hastings. The small church founded by that mission formed the foundation of the current cathedral. Known locally as Holy Rosary Cathedral, the imposing neo-Gothic church building sits in the heart of downtown Vancouver amidst the busy downtown shopping district with high-rise condos and office buildings all around. At the cathedral, a wide mix of ages and ethnicities come to worship, from downtown office workers in suits to the homeless. As one focus group participant said, "last week I saw the owner of the Vancouver Canucks hockey team in a pew beside a well-known and loved homeless woman who worships with us regularly. They were both there praising God together. That probably wouldn't happen in a suburban parish."

Archbishop J. Michael Miller is the head of the cathedral staff with another five priests and two permanent deacons ministering together downtown, offering three daily Masses, Monday to Saturday as well as four on Sunday, a Spanish-language Mass on Sunday evening, and a Latin Mass on Sunday afternoon that is described as "a celebration of the Latin Mass using the Missal antecedent to the reform of 1962 (Extraordinary Form/Tridentine Mass)." Other special services include a "Holy Hour and Happy Hour," providing worship and social

Figure 3.11 Historic Cathedral of Our Lady of the Holy Rosary
in downtown Vancouver

gathering time for young adults on Friday evenings, and many musical
concerts in the worship space. The cathedral is also home to ministries
such as Handmaids of the Lord (a Couples for Christ all-women's
ministry), the Knights of Columbus, and the Legion of Mary (lay
people who serve as prayer leaders, visit the sick, and evangelize).

In our interview at the cathedral, Father Nick Meisl reflected on his parish experiences throughout Vancouver and how common it was to lead a funeral for a devout Catholic grandparent whose adult children attended only at Christmas and Easter and whose grandchildren showed up to the funeral without any sense of the liturgy or the theological promises contained within. Fr Meisl's comments echo research on "lapsed Catholics" by Carol Ann MacGregor and Ashlyn Haycook who argue that "the most popular reason for leaving the Catholic Church is simply gradually drifting away from the religion" with the three main categories being "the injured," with negative experiences of church; "the drifter," struggling to see the difference faith made in their lives; and "the dissenter," actively disagreeing with the church teachings, particular around sexual morality.[63] As a Vancouver-born and raised Catholic, Fr Meisl is keenly aware that for many who were raised in a Catholic family, the practice of Christian faith within Roman Catholicism is a fading memory and thus the need for evangelization and mission is important. The focus group affirmed Fr Meisl's comments and named several Catholic mission groups, such as Catholic Christian Outreach and Couples for Christ, that are reaching out into the wider Vancouver context to share the gospel. Since Christopher James's research did not account for the unique characteristics of the Roman Catholic expression of Christian faith, it is difficult to connect the data from Holy Rosary with James's four typologies of church communities.

St Gregory the Illuminator Armenian Apostolic Church (Orthodox)

St Gregory the Illuminator Armenian Apostolic Church is located on the border between the city of Vancouver and the suburb of Richmond, near Vancouver International Airport. The facilities include a fellowship hall and language school, and many in the focus group commented on how it is not only their church but also their cultural and community centre. When asked what their relationship was to the surrounding (primarily Asian) neighbourhood in which the church is located, Father Karekin Shekherdemian and the focus group noted that there was almost no relational connection or mission engagement.[64] The website, in Armenian and English, describes the mission of the church as: "Spreading the light of Saint Gregory's inextinguishable lamp."[65] The leadership structure is clearly defined as episcopal,

Figure 3.12 St Gregory the Illuminator Armenian Apostolic Church

with a hierarchy from Archbishop Aram Keshishian down to the local parish priests. In the interview with Fr Shekherdemian, he noted the distinction that for Armenian Orthodox Christians their expression of faith is deeply tied to national or ethnic identity, something I observed while participating in their liturgy with its deep sense of tradition and adherence to Armenian customs and language, including the aesthetic of incense, candles, ringing of bells, icons, genuflecting, bowing, and kissing the altar.

In worship, conversation with the priest, and the focus group interview, the topic of human sexuality was not mentioned. There was a clear sense that this Christian community was set apart from the wider culture in language, custom, and practice. Of all the initiatives included in the fieldwork, St Gregory's appeared the least eager to engage the wider culture. In part, it was described as a minority position; as one focus group participant said, "our local church has a clear identity, and we are proud to be a part of the parish. For us, the survival piece is essential, living in Vancouver with a small population of Armenians here compared to the people around us." Another said: "The mission of the church in Vancouver is to spread the Word of God and to live a Christ-like life while living in a secular society that does not share those values – especially in a Western world where we live in a space where people believe such different things." There was, however, a sense of solidarity with others who experienced persecution and genocide, for example, partnering with the local Jewish community to mark the anniversary of the Armenian genocide together[66] as well as the connection with local First Nations groups to talk about reconciliation.

The focus of both St Gregory's witness and mission is directed to the Armenian diaspora in the Vancouver area – whether newly arrived immigrants or refugees or Canadian-born with Armenian heritage. Remarkably, the congregation (no more than one hundred in worship) has sponsored (or co-sponsored) one thousand Syrian refugees over the last decade to Vancouver. According to both Fr Shekherdemian and the focus group, this has revitalized the congregation and offered a clear sense of focus for mission through the ministry of hospitality and welcome. In conversation through this research, participants from St Gregory's reflected with appreciation on the impact of the newcomers on the community. Focus group participants suggested they have been so busy caring for refugees that they have not often had the time to stop and recognize how transformative it has been for the church. This experience in my fieldwork echoes the research by Helen Cameron and her colleagues where they note the importance of disclosing theology through a conversational method where the theological action research is "built on the conviction that the Holy Spirit is moving Christ's people to an ever deeper understanding of faith, in faith; and that this 'theology' is ever before us, waiting to be 'seen' or recognized."[67] Fr Shekherdemian did not downplay the challenge of reaching Canadian-born Armenians integrated into the broader secular culture, observing that some say, "I prefer to stay at home and pray." He counters with the need to be participating in the community: "I tell them that we are a family, and they need to be part of the family activities." Similar to the Roman Catholic site, the unique elements of this Armenian church meant that it falls outside of Christopher James's four typologies of church communities identified in his research in Seattle.

PARA-CHURCH AGENCIES

Sanctuary Mental Health Ministries

Sanctuary Mental Health Ministries was founded as a fee-based, in-person workshop for local churches in the Vancouver area to help raise awareness of mental health issues and provide a gospel-based response. By 2016, the original founders had moved on to other ministries and Daniel Whitehead was named executive director. He transformed the program to make it scalable and deliverable online by any small group leader, pitching it to his board by asking, "What would happen if all of our current facilitators of the Sanctuary course were hit by a bus? How would we continue?" It was a risky move, and not one without detractors, but the board authorized the change in model, and by 2016 the new Sanctuary course was available by download for a fee. Almost immediately the new model of delivery became popular, doubling the income of Sanctuary in a year and expanding its reach beyond the Vancouver area. Year after year, the Sanctuary course has grown, expanding into the United States and the United Kingdom. In late 2021, Archbishop of Canterbury Justin Welby became a patron, offering a huge boost to the ministry in the global Anglican Communion. The vision statement of Sanctuary is: "We envision a future where the Church plays a vital role in supporting mental health and wellbeing in every community." The mission is described as: "Sanctuary Mental Health Ministries equips the Church to support mental health and wellbeing."

As a Christian agency based in Vancouver, the space that Sanctuary inhabits is a virtual one. Sanctuary does not own any property and its Vancouver-based staff are deployed in their homes and neighbourhoods. Dan Whitehead spoke about the specific connection with Vancouver now that Sanctuary is a Christian agency with international scope. He noted that seventeen out of twenty staff members live in Vancouver, and that the majority of those downloading the Sanctuary course remain in the Lower Mainland region of British Columbia that includes Vancouver. "Vancouver is home for us, and it shapes the way we engage issues of faith, culture, and mental health," he said.

Sanctuary ministries does not align itself with a particular theological tradition. Instead, it describes its beliefs as "an ecumenical organization." However, it does tailor the online course offering to specific Christian audiences with a Sanctuary course for Catholics.

Figure 3.13   Sanctuary Mental Health Ministries small-group gathering for
a course

When reviewing the Sanctuary course, the first session includes the
statement, "This is why *The Sanctuary Course* was created: to raise
awareness and start conversations in local churches regarding mental
health. These are the primary goals of the course." Through video
interviews with theologians and church leaders as well as reflection
questions and small group discussion for those who download the
course, a conversational space is created where people's entry into
the topic of mental health and their Christian faith is grounded in
prayer.[68] The other sessions cover the topics of Mental Health and
Mental Illness, Stigma, Recovery, Companionship, and Self-Care
and the Church. Similar to the Catholic and Orthodox churches in
this book, Sanctuary as an ecumenical ministry with a particular focus
regarding mental health leaves it outside of James's four models identified in Seattle.

Online and in-person, Sanctuary Mental Health Ministries did not
address issues of human sexuality. As an ecumenical organization in
multiple countries that reaches congregations across the theological
spectrum for both services and fundraising, it may be that this is
intentional. Focus group participants, representing a mix of those who
worked for Sanctuary and those who have led the program in their

churches, were eager to engage in discussion on wider cultural political issues, including the environment and Indigenous issues. One participant pointed towards Sanctuary Ministries Healing in Colour project that invited BIPOC[69] persons, including Indigenous artists, to participate. The result was a huge surge in traffic to the Sanctuary website. "The compelling part of the project was really in the storytelling of the BIPOC and Indigenous community," noted one participant before adding the challenge, "so how do we engage Indigenous cultures and environmentalism as Christians in Vancouver through the specific practice of storytelling?" Another participant suggested that "the way we engage Indigenous culture, and the broader environmentalism movement, is to listen and give others a voice in the church. Too often historically the church was keen to speak on behalf of others with a uniform voice – we need to let go of our own pride and ego. Christians need to acknowledge we are no longer in control, and we can see God at work in others."

Sanctuary significantly increased its mental health ministry reach over the last five years, growing from a $100,000 budget in 2016 to a $1.5-million budget in 2021. Whitehead listed off all the different resources Sanctuary developed over the last few years, including the existing and soon-to-be-released new Sanctuary Mental Health course; a separate Sanctuary course for Catholics in English and Spanish; a podcast; resources for grief support; a COVID-19 stress resource; an Advent resource for those who struggle during the Christmas season; and partnerships with the University of Aberdeen in Scotland as well as Notre Dame University in the United States. Whitehead mentioned future projects in the works, including better Christian mental health resources for youth.

In the focus group discussion, participants spoke of both the necessity of engaging the topic of mental health and the connection points to the wider Vancouver culture. One participant said, "I dream that the unchurched would see the church as a place of welcome for those struggling with mental health concerns because community is such a part of health and well-being, and a lived spirituality with the Creator is important." Participants noted how mental health is widely discussed in Vancouver culture and viewed without stigma. Therefore, a particular mission of Sanctuary is to help bridge the gap between the church and the wider Vancouver society by connecting the scientific and spiritual worlds on mental health, as an essential part of Christian witness. In this sense, Sanctuary Mental Health Ministries is similar to the faith-based agencies studied by Helen Cameron and colleagues that were able to campaign, raise awareness, and seek to represent the voice of the churches to government and within the voluntary sector, while promoting innovative Christian responses.[70] Participants also acknowledged how Sanctuary encourages local churches to create space for discussion where people can admit that everything is not all right with their lives in order to address the reality of mental health struggles. One participant said, "Our way forward is to have a missional theology embraced by all the churches in Vancouver that is incarnational and holistic in its understanding of the gospel. If that could seep into the church across Vancouver, then we would see creation care and Indigenous culture more naturally addressed and embraced."

Jacob's Well

Jacob's Well is situated in Vancouver's Downtown Eastside neighbourhood beside the Community Health Centre and across from Oppenheimer Park, a well-known gathering place for homeless people and the location of a tent city that was removed in 2020 by city officials.[71] Jacob's Well has a bright and welcoming website with an introductory video to the ministry prominent on its landing page.[72] Founded in 2001 by an eighty-six-year-old member of the Downtown Eastside community named Pauline Fell, Jacob's Well reflects Fell's call to create a space that would reflect her Christian friendship-making ministry on the streets of the neighbourhood since 1976. Jacob's Well defines its mission as "radical welcome, showing love to all who come in the doors," with core values of hospitality, friendship/mutuality, spiritual formation, and pursuing justice guiding the community. Jacob's Well describes its identity as "a faith-based non-profit located in the Downtown Eastside of Vancouver" that seeks "mutually transformative friendship with those on the margins of society and [to] equip others to do the same in their own context." The ministry describes itself as an ecumenical Christian community: "We come from many different denominations and churches. We share the basics of the Christian faith, as defined in the Apostles' Creed, and we find unity around our commitment to Christ and to loving the people He loves. We strive to keep Christ at the centre of all we do."[73] Jacob's Well has a staff team of six that included Joben David as executive director and Aaron White as resident theologian.

Figure 3.14   Jacob's Well storefront ministry in the Downtown Eastside

As we walked through the neighbourhood and stopped for coffee in a diner, Aaron White talked about the challenge of having well-meaning Christians come into the Downtown Eastside to "serve" the homeless with sandwich handouts where people line up on one side of the table while volunteers put on gloves and stand on the other. White spoke passionately about the need to build genuine community where people were able to share life with one another. "If you want to feed someone a meal, have them into your home, build a real relationship with them – don't just give them a poor nutritional handout," he said. White talked about how at Jacob's Well he loves when people come into the community and are not able to easily discern who is living on the streets and who might be volunteering from a local church community. White described the ministries of Jacob's Well as including a social, relational, and spiritual dimension. Sharing life together, making meals, singing karaoke, playing ping-pong, studying the Bible, reading the newspaper, praying together all leads to a common life together.

I experienced this diversity and belonging that White described when I visited Jacob's Well for dinner and experienced people speaking freely and asking direct questions of me, such as "How old are you?" "Are you a pastor?" "Where do you live?" My dinner companions offered their own frank thoughts, including "I'm just recovering from COVID," "My friend just ended her life," "I heard on a radio program that the prophets were mini-incarnations of Jesus – what do you think?" The Wednesday night I arrived for the community meal, I entered a main room full of activity with about forty-five people present. Six large tables were set out with chairs around them. Someone sat on a sofa in the corner strumming a guitar and many people were already enjoying their dinner of grilled cheese sandwiches and tomato soup. The people in the room were a mix of ages and genders, with some young children also present. A member of the community greeted me and said that grace had already been offered, and I was welcome to grab some food and join them. Inside the kitchen, executive director Joben David was busy making grilled cheese sandwiches with volunteers from St Peter's Fireside. He greeted me warmly while buttering bread and invited me to sit wherever I like and join in conversation.

As I enjoyed my meal, I listened carefully to those around me, hearing their stories about living in the neighbourhood and asking questions about their experience at Jacob's Well. I noted that "God language" was freely and casually inserted into conversations in this space. People talked about God's activity in their lives, who they knew in the community who was sick or missing and how they were praying for them, and the churches they visited on a regular basis. This connected with Anna Strhan's research in London that found people were more comfortable talking about God in council estates than in middle-class spaces where "experiences of awkwardness signify a tension between the missionary norms encouraged through their church and a secularization of space that locates the religious within the realm of the personal."[74] Not long after I sat down to eat, two guitar players started strumming Christmas carols in the corner and the sound of so many people in conversation filled the room with a warm and inviting feeling.

After dinner I visited the prayer room that was decorated with many interactive prayer exercises. On one wall was a block-by-block drawing of the Downtown Eastside neighbourhood with all the different Christian missions and churches labelled. Index cards were jammed into various ministries – someone explained that people are invited to write down a prayer for these ministries, and once a month they are delivered like "greeting cards of grace." Another corner of the prayer room had bricks spread out on the floor, each one covered in writing. "We usually build those up into a wall," explained another person, "then we knock it down with prayers to remind us that Jesus breaks through any barrier." Every wall and corner was filled with similar interactive prayer activities for those who either dropped in to pray or gathered there for programs.

I asked about what everyday activities took place there and was told, "much of our life together is unplanned and random. We do everyday-life kind of things with our friends: we go shopping; we clean the bathroom; we help people move; we celebrate birthdays." The more "planned" activities of the community include prayer, where they draw on the new monastic text *Common Prayer: A Liturgy for Ordinary Radicals*, as well as providing a prayer room (as noted earlier) for anyone to use throughout the day. Another activity is games night, where the community gathers on Monday evenings for cards or boardgames and fellowship time together. On Wednesday and Thursday evenings, a community meal and worship are held as well. Social media accounts are active for Jacob's Well with both Facebook and Instagram, but the social media presence seems designed to connect people in-person at the ministry site rather than engage online. Jacob's Well demonstrated characteristics most similar with Christopher James's Neighborhood Incarnation model as a community- and mission-centred ministry where "the needs reveal the results of sin and brokenness that calls for healing ... and the hope is grounded in the belief that God is not finished there yet; God's Reign is yet to come in its fullness."[75]

In conversation with members of the Jacob's Well community, people were keen to share their background and tell me where they had lived before coming to Vancouver and the Downtown Eastside. They described Vancouverites outside of the Downtown Eastside as being private and "keeping to themselves." One person said, "everyone moves here to escape the snow from the rest of Canada," noting the shared experience that many in this city were born and raised somewhere else and how the mild winters and spending time outdoors is a common value. Another participant commented on how people always talk about how expensive Vancouver is with the cost of living and real estate – "that's something we have in common; no one can afford to live here."

EVALUATION

There is much to be gleaned from the rich data produced through the engagement of these fourteen Vancouver Christian initiatives. In particular, several general observations can be made on the fieldwork presented thus far.

First, both the walking interviews with pastors and the focus groups with lay people offer the perspective that, in the context of Vancouver, speaking with others in public about Christian beliefs is perceived to be challenging. In the wider culture a non-institutional spirituality may be present that includes attending to environmental stewardship and Indigenous culture, both of which were often named by participants early on without the researcher's prompting, yet Vancouverites remain in the "spiritual but not religious" mindset. This raises further questions about spirituality and social status in Vancouver, where a high cost of living, combined with pursuit of "the good life," and an outdoor lifestyle lead to individualistic spiritualities yoked to nature. Or as one focus group participant said, "when it comes to Vancouverites, walking through a rainforest or hiking a mountaintop is *their* cathedral." A common denominator in the fieldwork that helped with sharing Christian beliefs were pre-existing and meaningful relationships between Christians and those in the broader community. While there was evidence of more traditional forms of evangelism (talking to strangers and sharing religious tracts) among some of the ethnically specific congregations, most initiatives demonstrated a sharing of the gospel through existing networks of friendships in a friendly, non-coercive manner. This echoes Anna Strhan's study of evangelicals in London where she notes the tendency in "complex, differentiated societies ... to cope with the fragmentation of cultural spaces by compartmentalizing and separating religion out as discrete from other areas ... In such secular contexts, it feels 'unnatural' to talk about faith, as something felt to belong to a separate 'personal' sphere of life."[76] Missiologist Mechteld Jansen has also identified the challenge of engaging in faith talk with secular people when there is no longer a shared religious understanding in Western society. Jansen observes that "the shared context may be more or less tainted by memories of religion, artifacts, nostalgia, and painful reproaches. If anything, the shared context is marked by narrativity, authenticity, and a this-worldly orientation." Jansen suggests deep relationship and honest sharing is key, which "is why testimony, always involving the sincerity of the persons or groups that give this testimony, fits the actual task of mission more than reasoned apologetics alone."[77] Sociologist of religion Joel Thiessen at Ambrose University in Calgary found that Christians surveyed in Canada struggled with sharing their faith due to five key reasons: lack of confidence, increased antagonism or resistance to Christian values and the Christian church, fear of rejection, few non-believers as friends, and lack of training in articulating their faith to others.[78]

Second, the challenge of affordable housing and the persistent problem of isolation and loneliness in Vancouver appeared throughout the fieldwork. Participants identified the high cost of living and corresponding lack of affordable housing, along with the growing problem of isolation, loneliness, and mental health challenges, as mission opportunities for the church in Vancouver. Through a "counter-cultural" witness of sharing space and building deep relational communities of belonging, it was suggested the church has something to offer the wider culture through its gospel values that was not easily identifiable elsewhere in Vancouver.

Third, there was evidence of a different approach to mission between what might be called "progressive" and "traditional" churches. For example, it appears that the more progressive churches (mainline and those more inclusive on social issues such as LGBTQ+) tended to be newcomer focused, with an emphasis upon hospitality and creating a welcoming environment. These progressive churches bear the marks of what Christopher James calls either the New Community or Neighborhood Incarnation models that practise "their neighborhood-rooted spirituality and mission through significant personal and corporate commitments to local hospitality."[79] Traditional churches (including ethnic churches and those more conservative in theology) appeared to be more evangelistically driven, bearing some of the marks of James's Great Commission Team model that "understand their context as a spiritually dark and urgent mission field in need of their life-giving atonement-centred message."[80] Michael Wilkinson notes that evangelicals in Cascadia identify with this image of the region as a "mission field" that motivates them to engage in "a process of theological reflection, ministry evaluation, and contextualization of practice in relation to the predominately nonreligious population."[81] Also, the traditional churches appeared to be more proactive in sharing their Christian faith, in keeping with the Great Commission Team model, while progressive churches are more careful or hesitant in sharing Christian faith.

Fourth, the reputation of Christianity in Vancouver makes it challenging to engage more secular Vancouverites in mission. It was not just a lack of interest or indifference from those who might identify as "affable agnostic or angry atheist" but also the need to address and confess the past sins of the Christian church before even having the opportunity to engage others in witness. The perception of the church (whether progressive or traditional) by the wider public as a conservative organization that has done harm to LGBTQ+ and Indigenous peoples (through the Residential Schools program in particular) makes it challenging for Christians to engage in mission with others in the city. Here Anna Strhan's perception of the secular gaze is relevant with her suggestion that a Christian in the urban West today "not only speaks of her faith to non-Christians, but chooses to speak publicly of her faith in what is perceived as an oppressively secularist setting."[82]

Fifth, the face of Christianity appears to be changing in Vancouver due to immigration (primarily from Asia) with a growing impact of both ethnic-specific congregations and existing multi-ethnic congregations across the denominational spectrum. This shift is both questioning the value and meaning of traditional denominational identity where Roman Catholic may now mean Filipino rather than French Canadian, Christian Reformed may mean Chinese rather than Dutch, and Presbyterian may mean Taiwanese or Korean rather than Scottish. As noted in many of the focus group conversations, this non-European face of Christianity may prove to be an advantage for engaging Vancouverites, including Indigenous peoples, as BIPOC[83] Christians share their own stories of exclusion and struggle for acceptance in Western culture.

Sixth, the fieldwork identifies several examples of where the high cost of living and of real estate is impacting the way that Christians gather for worship and service in the city. The question of access to ecclesiastical space for new church plants, as well as how to repurpose existing ecclesiastical space (church buildings turning into condos), is a significant issue moving forward in Vancouver.

With these initial observations in mind, the next chapter draws more definitive conclusions from the fieldwork as we look towards normative outcomes answering our research question.

4

Learning from the Journey

Reflections upon Christian Witness in Vancouver

INTRODUCTION

In this chapter we turn to an evaluation of the data as we continue to address the research question, "How are Christians in Vancouver today, as a minority expression of the majority secular population, organizing their communities, shaping their beliefs, and expressing themselves in mission?" Our aim is to construct building blocks towards an urban missiological understanding of Canada's third-largest city. We examine the Vancouver data in light of an ongoing discussion with other scholars such as Noah Toly who ask, "How do we reckon with basic realities of cities – their physical form and relationship to nonhuman creation, their diversity, community, wealth and poverty, and their growing influence in the world – from a Christian perspective? What does it mean to develop a more informed and committed Christian perspective on urban life?"[1] Philip Sheldrake reminds us in his study of spirituality in urban contexts that "the contemporary diverse city is always provisional, in process of becoming, and necessarily the product of multiple negotiations on the street corner."[2] In reflecting on the journey we've just experienced through Vancouver's neighbourhoods and churches, clusters of data offer clues as to how Christians are organizing themselves for mission as they attempt to connect with Vancouverites who represent the broader, more secular urban culture. In this chapter, we explore seven significant observations emerging from the research that help us to better understand how Christians are organizing themselves and engaging the wider community in mission today. Each section below not only seeks to describe, summarize, and depict what Christian activity in Vancouver means but also seeks to set these observations within the wider North American missional church movement, in order to see how this research connects and contributes to the missional theology discourse grappling with Christian faith in a post-Christendom context.

I BEFRIENDING A "SPIRITUAL BUT NOT RELIGIOUS" CULTURE

An important observation in the fieldwork is that the data suggests many Christians in Vancouver struggle to speak their faith with others outside the local church context. Interview subjects repeatedly noted the "spiritual but not religious" mindset of their friends, neighbours, and co-workers that acknowledged a general, nature-based spirituality but resisted a more dogmatic expression of faith. Participants in this research described Vancouverites as sharing "a certain vague morality that is floating in the wider culture unattached to any particular religious tradition." An example suggested in one focus group was British Columbia provincial health officer Dr Bonnie Henry's liturgical refrain at the end of her pandemic press conferences: "Be calm, be kind, be safe."[3] This generic moralism now appears as street art, on T-shirts, and as the title of Dr Henry's autobiographical book. Others nodded in agreement and together the group noted how this generic morality is connected to another common value acknowledged as the spiritual but not religious belief in Vancouver. "Meditation, yoga, and 'finding oneself in the mountains' is everywhere," said one participant. "People are basically agnostic without any sense of being rooted to a tradition here," said another.

Here, the research in Vancouver echoed the findings of Elaine Graham who describes the "growing number of those who identify as 'spiritual but not religious' as an emergent new form of religious expression 'markedly more heterodox and personalized.'"[4] Recent research in the region has stated the challenge more bluntly: "Cascadians do not consider organized religion a necessary part of their lives."[5] In the fieldwork there was a clear sense of commitment by Christians to participation in God's mission in order to reach the city of Vancouver in general, as well as particular neighbourhoods or specific ethnic groups. The challenge seemed to be in how best to share the gospel with those in the city who acknowledged a spiritual but not religious mindset, but who would go no further, taking an affable

agnostic approach to organized religion, marked primarily by indifference. This research echoes that of Canadian sociologist of religion
Sarah Wilkins-Laflamme whose own study of British Columbians
revealed that the number of those identifying as atheists or secularist
was quite small compared to the largest number of those declaring
themselves "spiritual with no religion"[6] followed by "other non-
religion or nothing in particular" and "agnostic."[7] This is an important
distinction in the research, namely that the relational connections
between those who formally identify with religious institutions in
Vancouver and those residents who never have belonged to a faith
community could be described as apathetic rather than acrimonious.[8]
While other parts of North America may assume a more contentious
relationship between "believers and non-believers," marked for example by the rise of the New Atheists,[9] the Cascadian region that includes
Vancouver does not offer similar evidence. In reviewing the data on
how "nones" (those without affiliation to a religious tradition) self-
identify in British Columbia, sociologists Joel Thiessen and Sarah
Wilkins-Laflamme note the lower percentage that choose "atheist,
humanist or secularist" and suggest it is due to either an indifference
towards the labels and issues of religion by those raised in an irreligious
household on the West Coast or perhaps because the language of atheist "conjures up a negative stigma" of judging another's beliefs in a
Canadian society that values tolerance.[10] Sociologist of religion Nancy
Ammerman's research on the nones further complexifies the diversity
of the non-religious in North America society. Ammerman notes that
"if religion is something intertwined with multiple identities and sta-
tuses, disaffiliation is equally complex and deserves (equally) complex
attention."[11] As British Columbian scholar of religion Paul Bramadat
argues, "relations between the religious, spiritual and irreligious populations in the region strike me as remarkably congenial ... there is a
strong 'you do you' orientation in the region."[12] The very language of
"you do you" appeared throughout the focus group interviews in
Vancouver both as a statement of fact and as a frustration in not being
able to help Vancouverites who self-identified with a spiritual but not
religious worldview take further steps towards faith in Jesus. Focus
group participants from Artisan Church noted this challenge to
Christian witness in the city saying, "whenever faith comes up you
get the Vancouver chill,[13] where people are totally ambivalent to
Christianity. Instead, if people find out you're a Christian you get a
'you do you – follow your bliss' response." Another said: "The

post-Christendom nature of Vancouver is a hindrance, especially with younger people. People really don't know much about Christianity here, and what they know – they don't like."

This struggle for Vancouver Christians to articulate their faith as a witness to the broader community is consistent with other recent research on evangelism in Canada. Sociologist of religion Sam Reimer's research with evangelicals demonstrated a consistent hesitation to speak their faith in public, preferring instead to demonstrate their faith through action or "lifestyle evangelism" where "actions speak louder than words."[14] Canadian sociologist Joel Thiessen describes this distinction as "passive" and "active" evangelism, with passive evangelism taking the form of modelling Christian values without articulating faith beliefs.[15] If Canadian Christians are more hesitant to speak their faith in public in an act of witness, one wonders how they articulate their faith once others discover they are Christian. Several focus group participants from Holy Rosary Cathedral spoke to this. One said: "I find when people discover I'm a strong Catholic, it makes them curious, and they want to know more about what I believe and why." Another said: "All my work colleagues are not Christian, and so people are surprised when they find out I'm Catholic. They don't expect Catholics to be normal." One observed that "most Vancouverites care about the common good but are marked by a strong individualistic streak, and that adds to the challenge of connecting socially with others. That's why so many Vancouverites are lonely and don't know their neighbours, compared to other parts of the country that I've lived in." There was agreement on a shared value of being friendly but only to a point, and not overstepping others' privacy. "That's the Seattle freeze here in Vancouver," said one participant, describing the culture noted earlier of Vancouver's sibling city in Washington State where people are known to be friendly but cool towards others in social settings as identified in Christopher James's work.[16] One participant mentioned that a shared value was believing that life had some sort of purpose, however one might describe that using religious terms or more secular language. "Most of the people that I talked with, whether they are Christian or not, seem to have the same sense that we are all on this journey through life together, we are all connected in some way. We are all trying to find meaning and purpose in our lives." In all the focus groups, participants talked about how important existing relationships were to sharing Christian faith with others in Vancouver.

The Vancouver research echoes Hans Riphagen's study of Lunetten in the Netherlands, where a challenge to mission included both an absence of meaningful relationships between Christians and non-Christians, as well as a particular Christian frustration at how relationships almost never led to conversion. Riphagen writes that the experience of Christians in his research "shows that entering into relationships with people who are 'different' often becomes embroiled in a number of challenges; likewise pursuing meaningful relationships with neighbours often remains limited to adherence to the context-specific expectations associated with the 'neighbour-relation.'"[17] An example Riphagen offered from his research, that resonated in the Vancouver focus group conversations, was of a Christian in Lunetten named Kees, who had high ideals of building meaningful relationships with neighbours. But after joining a local homeowner's association and engaging in practices such as faithfully attending meetings, staying after to help clean up, and joining in small talk, Kees described his "witness" as a failure. As Riphagen notes, Kees's "missional theology of building meaningful relationships with neighbours (perhaps a first step of finding an opening for the gospel), seems to invalidate the value of *ordinary* neighbourliness."[18] Participants in the Vancouver research expressed similar disappointment and frustration that engagement with their non-Christian neighbours so rarely led to deeper conversations (let alone occasions of conversion). For example, while walking with Pastor Sterne of St Peter's Fireside, he described how difficult it was to build relationships with neighbours in downtown Vancouver. Living previously in a high-rise condo, it seemed almost impossible to connect, even with those on the same floor. Now living in a low-rise townhouse complex, Sterne shared stories of more recent connections with neighbours. He noted that it took several years for meaningful conversation to happen with neighbours in a city where people are often highly transient and never stay put long enough to have that kind of break-through connection. Focus group participants from many initiatives described the challenge of encountering Vancouver neighbours with no religious tradition that made their own faith-based practices seem strange. Participants noted that the Christian practices and beliefs of church members (described by one as their "piety and devotion") stood at odds with those living in the neighbourhood who were spiritual but not religious and could be seen happily out cycling, jogging, pushing strollers, or meeting in coffee shops when worship was taking place. One participant said with a sigh, "there is no sense in our more secular neighbours that what we do and believe might be something that they need or want in their lives." This was also echoed by participants in the Armenian Orthodox focus group who struggled to understand their neighbours who could so easily separate out religion and spirituality: "People talk about being spiritual not religious, but what does that mean? Organized religion has a bad reputation and as Armenian Christians we see religion and spirituality as one, but most of our neighbours don't see them together." Another added: "People in my neighbourhood talk about having good energy, in a New Age sense, where we talk instead about God. How do we find those connection points with Christianity when our neighbours talk about meditation, but we talk about prayer?" To that point, another participant said: "It's not a city where people are open to sharing faith. I think it would be strange to start a conversation with someone else about faith here. In Vancouver, it's frowned upon to discuss your beliefs, as it is seen as a challenge to our values of diversity and inclusivity."

Despite these challenges of living and sharing the gospel as a "sent" community of Christians in Vancouver, the research offered evidence of effective engagement with the broader, more secular urban context. While conversations with some Christian leaders suggested that clergy had greater urgency than their parishioners in reaching out to Vancouverites, the focus group participants consistently demonstrated both a desire to reach out to neighbours and a commitment to the common task of clergy and lay to engage in mission. As one focus group member said: "Our mission is to include everyone and spread God's love and we are all the same as human beings. Wherever we are in the city, whatever we are doing for work or play, we are involved in loving the other just as we love God." For example, in conversation with Pastor Dan Matheson of Tenth Kits, he reflected on the challenge of mission to more secular neighbours in the Kitsilano area, noting that very few people just "wandered in off the street." Instead, the growth of the church was due to relational connections with neighbours, again reflecting the Neighborhood Incarnation model of treating neighbour as subject rather than object.[19] Pastor Matheson himself articulated the many ways that he has worked, and equipped members of Tenth Kits, to engage in the local neighbourhood, from being in the same coffee shop to volunteering for community associations to service projects for the common good. The leadership style offered by Pastor Matheson echoed research by the Presbyterian

Church (USA)'s 1001 New Worshiping Communities project that describes effective missional leaders as those who "enter a neighbourhood with the intention of listening and learning about that neighborhood from those who are already invest in the well-being of the neighbourhood. They spend time in restaurants, libraries, gyms, basketball courts, schools, and shops, knitting connections with people and the activities that engage the people of the neighborhood. It is out of those relationships that community grows."[20] Pastor Matheson and members of the focus group from Tenth Kits described how these practices of neighbourhood engagement brought members of the community into the fellowship. "People have joined Tenth Kits over the years," he reflected, "because their co-worker said, 'Hey, our church has a great kids' program that would be good for your family,' or they say to a neighbour, 'You should come to church and hear my pastor speak, he helps make sense of things in my life and the world.'" Focus group participants noted several outreach activities, and all agreed that being part of a multi-site congregation like Tenth Church meant that their individual expression of Christian community benefited from connection with the larger organization with various outreach programs. Participants identified the challenge of sharing Christian faith with others in Vancouver and named deep relationships with others, despite their varied beliefs, as a priority for mission in Vancouver. Participants also noted that traditional viewpoints on human sexuality, as well as scandals and hypocrisy in the church, factored into what hinders Christians from sharing their faith.

Specifically, the research demonstrated that Christians in Vancouver articulate a great emphasis upon building relationships with their non-Christian neighbours in order to attempt to share and show the gospel. As one focus group participant said, "the most helpful thing in the end is forming relationships with deep care and trust – you don't come into people's lives with an agenda, instead you come with love." In other words, evangelistic witness without a pre-existing friendship or relationship did not prove effective for many. While evangelistic street outreach does happen in Vancouver, those interviewed for this book consistently named the priority of building relationships with family, friends, co-workers, and neighbours as a place for mutual sharing of values and beliefs. The research revealed that this kind of relationship building was not programmatic but rather encouraged theologically in the teaching of the local churches and left to happen organically (whether or not it actually happens in practice) as church members lived their lives at work and in the neighbourhood. As one focus group participant said, "it helps when Christians are genuinely excited about the good news and share it organically through their life and relationships, rather than as a pre-packaged program."

This was evident in the data, with Christians speaking consistently of being an "alternative community" and a "countercultural witness" in Vancouver, primarily by offering evidence of lives changed through a hospitable common life together, suggesting it was unlike anything found in other non-profit organizations in the city.[21] However, the language of "countercultural" raises further questions as it can sometimes be used in a post-Christian setting to idealize the small community of faith and demonize the wider, more secular culture. As Stefan Paas argues, "the term 'counter-cultural' must be used with great care, as it can easily lead to rather misguided and even destructive conceptualizations of the relationships between church and world."[22] Paas suggests that churches seeking to be "really missional in a post-Christian world ... must abandon timeless, supra-cultural constructions of the relationship between church and world – either theocratic or counter-cultural. Something is wrong with a Christian identity if it depends on almost entirely negative (or optimistic, for that matter) depictions of the world."[23] The "intensifying" nature of Christian community was discernible in a number of the initiatives, as Christians sought to form deeper bonds with each other (including hospitality to strangers) in light of the self-understanding of being a minority people in a larger, majority non-Christian Vancouver culture. Here Canadian missional leader Preston Pouteaux's concept of Christians being a "keystone people" fits well. When speaking to Vancouver pastors at St Andrew's Hall in January 2022, Pouteaux used his experience from beekeeping in Chestermere, Alberta, to describe keystone species as animals that often go unnoticed but have a key role in their context, just as a bee pollinates flowers. Without the keystone species, so many others could not thrive. Vancouver pastors at the event told me afterwards that the image of the church Pouteaux went on to describe as a small community made up of keystone people resonated deeply with their experience of Christian life and witness in the city. Pouteaux cautioned the pastors that Christians as keystone people is a different concept than Christendom era's Christians as pillars of the community. Instead, drawing on his writing, Pouteaux cautioned that keystone people may not be the most noticeable or celebrated, but they are essential to the neighbourhood.

Questions to ask are: "Do I, as a pastor and neighbour, move about my neighbourhood slowly, attentively, patiently, and with a focus to bring life? Do I make things beautiful? Do I ensure that others benefit from the life I lead? Do I start my day intent on leaving it better than I found it? Do I work with others to find creative ways of helping my city thrive? Am I a keystone person?"[24] Indeed, based on the data, Pouteaux's keystone people were evident in the Vancouver research sites as they tried to connect their faith in community with the wider, secular context of Vancouver. As evidence, the following six sections explore how Christians in Vancouver perceive they are trying to make the gospel comprehensible through relationships to the wider, waiting, and watching world.

This initial observation of how Vancouver Christians struggled to find an effective connection with their non-Christian, and often secular, neighbour connects to the larger missional church conversation's emphasis on the concept of witness. Darrell Guder argues that a key concept defining a missionally alert church is that of witness. "The basic New Testament term (the root is *martus*, martyr) aptly captures the core reality of the missional ... church: the witness is a person whose life provides evidence of the gospel that God's Spirit uses for its purposes. Such persons drawn into community present their witness (*marturia*) before a watching world. Thus, their life corporately and individually is a process of witnessing (*marturein*) that the Spirit uses to draw others into the service of Christ."[25] The Christian initiatives studied in this research reflect ideas and self-understanding similar to what Guder describes in more formal theological language: Christians seeking to be a witness as a minority expression of belief in a wider, more secular Vancouver society.[26]

The priority on personal relationships for missional engagement that emerged from the Vancouver data echoes a recent study by Bryan Stone that identified how a relationship with a Christian is the number one reason people connect with Christianity. For example, three-quarters of those surveyed by Stone identified a partner or spouse, a church community, friend, family member, or minister as the main influence on their decision to become a Christian.[27] Christian witness, a key theme in the ongoing missional theology discussion, is rooted firmly in this research through the deep, personal, and ongoing relationships between Vancouver Christians and their non-Christian neighbours, family, and friends. This emphasis in the data of Christians focusing on (some focus groups used the phrase "investing in") deep relationships with Christian and non-Christian friends is consistent with Andy Root's argument that "even in an immanent frame, the concrete place where people testify to encountering the presence of the living Christ is in resonant actions of relationships, which avoid the temptation of expending energy and instead just be."[28]

A question remains regarding how Christian leaders, drawing on missional theology, are instructing and equipping their initiative members to engage with their non-Christian neighbours. Missional theology places an emphasis upon joining God in the local neighbourhood, what Joel Thiessen describes as a "qualitative concentration"[29] on a particular group of people and place, and there are those within the missional church movement in North America who advocate for a more formal encouragement of Christians to practice the "art of neighbouring."[30] Canadian missional practitioners such as Preston Pouteaux encourage churches to help their members discover the particular neighbouring gift they have, such as the celebrator (on the hunt for good news), the repairer (keen to mend and make things right), the de-stressor (bringing calm and peace), the activator (someone who gets things going), the caregiver (quietly attending to hurt in the community), the includer (speaking well of others and encouraging participation of all), and the discoverer (on the lookout for new ideas and possibilities for the neighbourhood).[31] Pouteaux's categories are helpful but can feel a little aspirational in Vancouver, easier to embrace as missional rhetoric rather than missional practice. While there are Christians such as Barry Jung (a layperson), who has become well-known in the church and community for his community garden project and outspoken advocacy for community engagement,[32] many in this research struggled for meaningful connection with others. Participants expressed frustration regarding how to connect with their neighbours, with one saying, "Vancouverites value leisure – like a beer commercial where you go skiing *and* golfing on the same day here in the city. People here love to run down Toronto as the working city." It was noted by participants that people in Vancouver attached a core value, even a theological one to leisure. "Leisure is the god of Vancouverites," observed another participant. That includes "the good life," whether it is the cars people drive, the vacations they take, or the high-end food they eat. How do you engage neighbours with a faith that prioritizes self-sacrifice in a culture of leisure?

Further research will be needed to probe whether the call to engage with neighbours is more a formal ideology confessed by pastors and theologians than an actual practice undertaken by Christians in their everyday lives. Here again, Hans Riphagen's study in the Netherlands is a helpful conversation partner, with his observations that Christians in his research lacked a theology of ordinary neighbourliness. Riphagen described evangelical Christians in his study as having an instrumentalized understanding of neighbour engagement focused on evangelism that resulted in a "mental block" that paralyzed people from "more informal and casual interaction."[33] Riphagen summarizes the challenge by asking how churches can "foster viable and positive legitimations of mission, that move beyond the 'mission is evangelism as recruitment' deadlock" while at the same time noting that "the absence of narratives of conversion, of successful authentic evangelism or faith transmission remains in itself an uneasy and unsolved challenge."[34] A local example of a prominent Vancouver Christian leader addressing this theme is Ken Shigematsu, pastor of Tenth Church and a popular speaker across Canada in missional circles, who encourages church members to invest in long-term friendships with neighbours for the sake of their faith development. He writes that "when we have a little free time, we may be inclined to use that time for social media or watching Netflix, which also promises immediate gratification. Cultivating relationships with friends and family members, by contrast, often requires years of investment, and we usually don't see immediate results." We are left to presume that the intended "results" are a conversion experience to Christianity. Pastor Shigematsu continues: "For most people friendship does not feel like an urgent priority. But if friendships are truly important to us, we will take the initiative to cultivate them. It's one thing to say we value relationships, but this doesn't mean anything if we don't take action."[35] Again, here we are left to presume that "most people" means Christians (in his church) and that friendship is meant to be the proactive work of a Christian seeking out a connection with their neighbour (family or friends). But does this kind of instruction from Christian leaders take on flesh in the ordinary, everyday lives and practices of church members? As well, in a context like Vancouver, where many residents are on their third or fourth generation raised without religion, this study identified the challenge of sharing faith even *within* established relationships. Further research will be required to explore the connection between the more formal or ideal theological encouragement for neighbour engagement versus the actual challenge of practice identified by Riphagen as including the danger of making the neighbourhood a normative everyday life for all, presenting the neighbourhood as a neutral social space, and representing "localism" as a desired simplification of otherwise fragmented and mobile lives.[36]

This emphasis upon relationship is being recognized more widely in the Canadian missional church discussion as missiologist Lee Beach, at McMaster University in Hamilton, Ontario, notes that missional relationships "call us to be listeners and caregivers in a way that embodies with care the compassion of God himself. It asks us to, like Jesus, be willing to be found with the 'sinners' and the unlovely so that the relational priorities of God are found in our lives too. Furthermore, this kind of relational evangelism means that the church itself will function as a place that demonstrates the power of Christ to transform human relationships."[37] Sam Reimer and Michael Wilkinson note that Christians engaging in the missional church movement "seek to take the church back to Jesus' mission to reach their community and world. They focus on the needs external to the church by incarnating Christ to their neighbours, and are less focused on needs and program development inside the church."[38] In Alberta, theologian Gordon Smith at Ambrose University notes that "we cannot in the end be spiritual without being religious. Authentic spirituality needs the sustaining power of a community with a shared faith, conviction, orientation, and accountability. Religious belief is inherently communal."[39]

2 AFFORDABLE HOUSING
AS A MISSIONAL CONNECTION

It doesn't take long to be in conversation with Vancouverites before the topic of real estate and affordable housing comes up. Housing is a major social issue affecting the quality of life for residents, with Vancouver ranked the second-most expensive city in the world to live in, behind only Hong Kong at the time of this study.[40] The average price of a detached home in Vancouver is around $1.8 million.[41] Part of the challenge in Vancouver's housing market is the issue of investment income entering the city from overseas, commonly seen as foreign buyers affecting a domestic market. For example, the *Vancouver Sun* profiled the majority owner of a mansion in Point Grey (a neighbourhood within this study) that was sold by Canaccord founder Peter Brown for a record $31.1 million to a "student." In 2016, land title documents listed Tian Yu Zhou as having a 99-per-cent interest in the five-bedroom, eight-bathroom, 14,600-square-foot mansion on a 1.7-acre lot at 4833 Belmont Avenue. Zhou's occupation was listed as a "student."[42]

Stories like this have increased local frustration with the lack of affordability in Vancouver. Eveline Xia, a resident of Vancouver's Mount Pleasant neighbourhood, took to Twitter to express anger at the city's housing crisis. Xia started #DontHave1Million to protest how unaffordable home ownership had become, as Statistics Canada data shows, a net loss of residents aged twenty to thirty years old from the Vancouver area as they move to more affordable communities across the country.[43] It is important to note, however, that the current reality regarding real estate is, in part, the outcome of Canadian policy regarding overseas investment over several decades. Following the recession of the early 1980s, both the Liberal federal government and the Social Credit provincial government in British Columbia sought ways of rebooting the economy on the West Coast by marketing British Columbia as an investment destination. Dubbed the "Pacific Strategy," it involved all levels of government courting investment from Asia as one of the fastest growing economies in the world, particularly China.[44]

Of course, the growing gap between rich and poor in the city is not just an economic question but also a social one. Greater Vancouver is famous for being home to Canada's wealthiest postal code (West Vancouver) and Canada's poorest (Downtown Eastside). As Douglas Coupland described the odd reality: "Heroin is a given. The corner of Main and Hastings is in the poorest postal code in Canada and is home to untold social ills, not the least of which is smack. Adding to its weirdness is its close proximity to perky, cruise-liner friendly Gastown, and to fastidious Chinatown."[45]

More recently, the introduction of fentanyl, which resembles heroin but is one hundred times stronger, has prompted an opioid crisis claiming the lives of over fifteen hundred British Columbians a year, with many of those deaths in Downtown Eastside.[46] Emergency workers in that neighbourhood have responded to as many as 130 overdose calls in one day with fatalities as high as 11 deaths in a twenty-four-hour period.[47] As one community leader remarked, "the overdose crisis indicates the amount of pain, trauma, and isolation many experience (and try to self-medicate). We are a rich city, yet too many suffer hunger, homelessness, etc."[48]

Throughout this research into Christianity in Vancouver, the question of affordable housing was named as a challenge and, for some, an opportunity for mission. "In Vancouver there is a lot of need regarding affordable housing and in terms of support for immigrants and those facing poverty, addictions, and other challenges. That's where the church needs to be," suggested one focus group in the study. As well, the connection of affordable housing to hospitality, while serving the needs of the city and engaging the neighbourhood, became clearer in the walking conversations with pastoral leaders and in the fourteen focus groups. Participants named specific non-profit organizations in Vancouver with whom they supported addressing the issue of affordable housing, including More Than a Roof Housing Society, Kinbrace Refugee Housing and Support, Baptist Housing, and Youth Unlimited. Others named the ways in which they were engaging with politicians, the media, and property developers to advocate for more affordable housing in the city. In addition to advocacy and support for the provision of affordable housing, Christian initiatives such as Tapestry–Marpole specifically identified how they were engaging in missional action and building relationships with those living in afford-able housing projects in their neighbourhood. Pastor Jesse Pals of Tapestry–Marpole noted the mutual benefit of these missional engage-ments with affordable housing where the experience of connecting through a common meal and social activities afterwards provided "an opportunity to share life and love with our neighbours. It is a trans-formative impact on our members." The focus group praised the relational connections from this missional activity while noting the challenge of sharing Christian faith with others in Vancouver. They observed that a conversation partner with a background in Christian faith was an asset in Vancouver. "For example," said one participant, "if they grew up going to church, the conversation starts in a different place. You don't have to explain certain basic concepts." All agreed that a pre-existing friendship or relationship with a person made a sig-nificant difference in the openness the other had to hearing a Christian's viewpoint in a conversation. The congregation's relationship with the affordable housing project helped create those deeper relationships for witness. Pastor Pals described the importance of preparing volunteers from Tapestry–Marpole to not see this as a soup kitchen, but as an opportunity to share life and love with their neighbours. Focus group participants also named Reiderman Residence[49] as their primary mis-sion engagement with the neighbourhood over the last several years. Participants had personal experience of making meals and sharing life with people in the affordable modular housing project. Focus group participants reflected on how much they learned spending time with disadvantaged neighbours and sharing the love of Jesus in simple acts. After these meetings the team would often go for a walk together or stop at a coffee shop and debrief their experiences with Pastor Pals. Pastor Pals himself referenced the importance of engaging in this shared practice with church members of serving at Reiderman and then taking time to theologically reflect together afterwards. This practice of theological action and reflection with a mentor is supported by James Heft in his studies of missional engagement with youth and young adults. Drawing on his Catholic faith, Heft writes that "Pope Paul VI once wrote that while we need witnesses more than teachers, what we most need is teachers who are witnesses. These witnesses need to listen and then teach. Pope Francis has repeatedly emphasized the importance of 'accompaniment,' which requires mentors to listen and teach, as Jesus did on the road to Emmaus."[50]

Another example was Rev. Trevor Vanderveen at First Christian Reformed Church who stressed the central role that the church's proximity to the affordable housing project for immigrants has had on his congregation. As he showed me around the church building, Rev. Vanderveen explained that the balcony of the sanctuary was converted to house clothing for refugees arriving in Canada without any supplies and living across the street in temporary housing. As we walked out of the church building, on our way to a local coffee shop, he stressed that the relationship with the refugee centre next door has been an essential part of the congregation's understanding of mission in the neighbourhood. He explained that when the centre was first built, the non-profit leaders were wary of the church's desire to become involved, fearing they were going to proselytize. Instead, Rev. Vanderveen assured the organization's leaders that they were there to provide a ministry of hospitality. Dena, the classis (regional judicatory) refugee chaplain based in the congregation, had lived in Egypt and speaks Arabic, which has been helpful with many refugees arriving from the Middle East with an Islamic background. Rev. Vanderveen pointed out that the older homes around the church are now – as in many neighbourhoods of Vancouver – worth more than $1.5 million each. In First Reformed Church's focus group it was noted that Christian mission with affordable housing was not simply providing a place to live but impacting the quality of life through healthy, gospel-based relationships. As one participant said, "affordable housing is not just about hospitality for the poor or at-risk street population.

Hospitality goes further because Vancouver is so lonely and expensive, the church needs to build community where it is lacking." In Kitsilano Christian Community both Pastor Monica McKinlay and members of the focus group affirmed the urgency for Vancouver churches to engage with the housing crisis. One participant remarked that "in Vancouver there is a lot of need regarding affordable housing and in terms of support for immigrants and those facing poverty, addictions, and other challenges. That's where the church needs to be."

Often, affordable housing is seen from a Christian perspective as "care for the poor"; however, an important dimension of the affordable housing debate in Vancouver is that it is difficult to afford housing in the city even for those with financial means. For example, a recent survey of the broader Cascadian region echoes this book's focus on affordable housing as a key issue: as University of Victoria scholar Paul Bramadat notes, "the cost of living in the region has become one of the galvanizing concerns animating younger urban residents. These worries are by far most acute in Vancouver and Seattle, where, for a variety of reasons, it is difficult for many young people – even educated professionals – to imagine ever owning a home."[51] To that end, the United Church of Canada has proposed a partnership with the British Columbia government to build four hundred new affordable rental homes for individuals, families, and seniors at four church-owned properties (three in Greater Vancouver and one on Vancouver Island), for people with average annual incomes between $50,000 and $100,000.[52] That someone earning $100,000 a year would qualify for "affordable housing" illustrates Bramadat's point that there is a crisis in housing in the region extending throughout different parts of society.

The missional church conversation places a great emphasis upon the local context as the primary place of both encountering the Divine and demonstrating love of God and neighbour. With a frequent call to "join God in the neighbourhood" and corresponding invocation of Jeremiah 29 to seek the peace and prosperity of the city where believers reside, attention to the specific social concerns of Vancouver is an essential aspect for developing a robust, urban missiological understanding.

From the research, we see Christian initiatives taking their local context seriously by paying attention to the specifics of what makes their neighbourhood a place of God's revelation and context for mission. Consistently, the challenge was named by participants in this study of both the affordable housing crisis and the persistent problem of isolation and loneliness in Vancouver. Indeed, social isolation is deeply rooted

in the region, given its historic self-identification with rugged individualism. People moved here from other places in North America to escape
commitments to social or religious institutions as documented by scholars such as Lynn Marks. Historically, with employment and riches in
the region provided by nature's bounty, "many residents of Cascadia
learned it may not have been a Supreme Being – but sheer hustle, luck
and location, location, location (exemplified in the real estate boom) –
that determined whether one fell by the economic wayside or joined the
economic elite."[53] There is a social cost to this rugged individualism,
however. In its well-researched, detailed, and thoughtful 2012 report,
the Vancouver Foundation released its findings regarding social isolation
for residents, entitled "Connections and Engagement."[54] The foundation funded research that included interviews with nearly four thousand
local citizens from over eighty different ethnic groups as well as two
hundred and seventy-five non-profit organizations and one hundred
notable community leaders. The research discovered that:

1   Metro Vancouver can be a hard place to make friends.[55]
2   Our neighbourhood connections are cordial, but weak.[56]
3   Many people in Metro Vancouver are retreating from
    community life.[57]
4   There are limits to how people see diversity as an opportunity
    to forge meaningful connections.[58]
5   The affordability issue in Metro Vancouver is affecting people's
    attitudes and beliefs.[59]

The report gained significant media attention and challenged the
prevailing notion that Vancouver was somehow a friendly city made
up of distinct neighbourhoods with character and culture. When asked
where home is, Vancouverites may identify with a particular neighbourhood such as "Kits" or "East Van," but the data suggested they
did not identify with their *particular neighbours*.

In other words, Vancouverites might readily connect with their
specific *place* in the city, without connecting with the particular *people*
who inhabit that shared space. A 2017 follow-up report by the
Vancouver Foundation discovered that respondents were less likely to
be involved in community life than when surveyed five years earlier.
The reason why had shifted slightly, from most respondents saying that
"they had nothing to offer" the wider community to now reporting
that "they did not have enough time."[60] Canadian Broadcasting

Corporation producer Jennifer Wilson followed up on the second survey looking at the demographic identified between the ages twenty-five and thirty-five and how they were impacted by social isolation. Wilson interviewed young adults who told her, "I haven't made a new friend in Vancouver since university, and I graduated nearly a decade ago. My few friends moved away, and I really haven't had a friend here for the past six or so years." Another young adult interviewed named Chris Monk identified the crisis of isolation in terms of existential angst saying, "I was raised in Ottawa and in France, and Vancouver is, without a doubt, a city with no soul. People are polite and friendly but that's as far as it goes. There is no depth whatsoever."[61]

The *Guardian* newspaper in London also picked up on the theme of isolation in Vancouver and published an article in 2017 asking whether Vancouver was unique in loneliness or simply better at recognizing it? Some, such as David Beattie, a South African who moved to Vancouver in 1988, are quick to assert that Vancouver is in a class of its own. "I've lived in six countries on four continents. And it's clear that even compared to London, Vancouver is disengaged," Beattie said. "People don't call you back, people don't invite you out, they don't make eye contact."[62] He pointed to a mix of factors to explain the issue, from Vancouver's rainy climate to the high cost of living and the language and cultural barriers that at times spring up among the city's diverse population.

Far from seeing these challenges as somehow separate from the Christian communities in Vancouver, interview subjects often identified the high cost of living and corresponding lack of affordable housing, along with the growing problems of isolation, loneliness, and mental health challenges, as clear missional responsibilities for the church in the city. For example, in a recent publication, Pastor Tim Dickau reflected on his thirty-year leadership of Grandview Church in East Vancouver and the congregation's commitment to affordable housing by developing both "Kinbrace," a home for refugees awaiting their government hearing, and "Co:here," a multi-storey housing complex built on the church parking lot. The missional impetus for this work came about as "our church faced another issue connected to the land as we have witnessed gentrification and the rising costs of housing in our neighbourhood and city. In cities with gross wealth inequalities, renters are particularly vulnerable, especially those with a fixed or low income ... the change in the selling price of detached homes in Vancouver rose from just under $400,000 in 2001 to $1,826,541 in 2016. This inflationary spike created a housing crisis across Vancouver."[63]

From advocacy for more affordable housing and creative use of church assets for housing development to the heavy emphasis on hospitality and friendship in Christian community, the research identified a variety of ways in which this pressing issue was being seen as a missional opportunity. This is not without challenge, however, as Jonathan Bird from Union Gospel Mission noted at a recent affordable housing conference. He said that there are only a little over two hundred church buildings left in the city of Vancouver, many of which are located on small lots in residential areas, making their land unsuitable for such redevelopment.[64] Nevertheless, the desire to provide affordable housing as a missional engagement with the city and the intention to provide hospitality and build deeper relationships with isolated and lonely neighbours came through clearly in the data. Acting as a counter-cultural witness, participants suggested that the church has something to offer the wider culture through its gospel values that was not easily identifiable elsewhere in Vancouver. This emphasis in the data of Vancouver Christians engaging the issue of affordable housing as a missional action, raises the question of where else across Canada might this also be found?

3 DISCERNING MODELS OF CHRISTIAN WITNESS

As noted throughout this book, the Vancouver research began in the wake of the significant work completed by Christopher James in *Church Planting in Post-Christian Soil* further south in the Cascadian region. Focusing on church plants in Seattle, Washington, for the first decade and a half of the twenty-first century, James developed four models of new Christian communities – Great Commission Team, Household of the Spirit, New Community, and Neighborhood Incarnation. James's research produced heuristic models of new churches and characteristics of their engagement with the city of Seattle. While James focused on the characteristics of community present in these new churches, this research expanded the scope to include a wider sample of mainline Protestant, neighbourhood-focused, large multi-site campuses, ethnically specific churches, Orthodox/Roman Catholic, and para-church agencies, in addition to church plants.

Similar to James's findings, the Vancouver data offered evidence of a strong emphasis upon community and belonging, with many of the initiatives studied reflecting the characteristics of the Neighborhood Incarnation model (St Peter's Fireside, First Christian Reformed Church, Tapestry–Marpole). As one focus group participant said, "what helps is our deep Christian community in this city that has a loneliness epidemic. People see what we have, and they think, 'Hey, I need that too.'" Some of the sites visited reflected a shared emphasis upon welcome, hospitality, and community but leaned more towards the New Community model with their particular emphasis upon LGBTQI inclusion (Artisan Church, Oakridge United Church, Kitsilano Christian Community, St Paul's Anglican Church). As one focus group participant said, "we're known and trusted in the community. Being known in the community as a LGBTQI inclusive church helps in conversations with others, since they often presume that most Christians are judgmental towards those of different sexual orientations." This emphasis on trust is important in a context where the church faces multiple challenges for connection with secular Canadians, as Michael Daly notes: "increasing secularization, the proliferation of modern spiritual practices, and the church's very public mistreatment of Indigenous Canadians, LGBTQ2S individuals, women, and other marginalized groups has caused the church to be suspect in the eyes of many."[65]

While the data in this Vancouver research suggests that the Neighborhood Incarnation model (and the New Community to a lesser extent) are present in the city, this does not deny the presence or impact of James's other models, Household of the Spirit and especially Great Commission Team, with some evidence present in the more theologically conservative churches. For example, Chinese Presbyterian Church offered amble evidence of traditional evangelistic outreach in the community. Focus group participants were keen to share stories of their personal evangelistic outreach with co-workers and neighbours in the city. It was agreed that what helps in sharing Christian faith is when believers are engaged relationally with others and able to address their needs. "In order to talk about faith in Vancouver, people need to know you and know that you really care," said one participant. Others said that what helps in speaking Christian faith in Vancouver is simply being bold and starting conversations with others. It was suggested that Christians are often too afraid of offending people by speaking about the faith, when really many people in a post-Christendom context like Vancouver are quite open to at least discussing faith and spirituality. "What really helps," said one participant, "is being bold and authentic in your witness – tell and show others in your life that God loves them, and that God cares for them." Here, Chinese Presbyterian Church offered examples of James's Great Commission Team model: "sent with a limited task on a comprehensive scale (evangelization ... of all nations)."[66]

Despite the wider field of study in the Vancouver research beyond church plants, the Christian initiatives displayed a common appreciation for organizing themselves to be places of welcome and hospitality, attentive either to a particular ethnic group (Armenian Orthodox, Chinese Presbyterian), neighbourhood (Kitsilano Community Church, Tapestry–Marpole), or the wider city (Sanctuary Mental Health Ministries, Holy Rosary Cathedral). Here, the Vancouver data echoes other recent research in the region, including Dustin Benac's examination of the Parish Collective in Seattle and Office of Church Engagement in Spokane, Washington. Benac notes that in the Pacific Northwest a high value is placed on idealism, autonomy, and self-expression, which presents challenges for connection in what he calls "the wake of institutions." Benac writes that "as a result, organizational adaptations in religious organizations and leadership emerge from a context where individuals are ambivalent about inherited templates for tradition-bound religious organizations and desire connection that occurs in – but also beyond – the traditional boundaries of organized religious life."[67] These adaptations were evident in the Vancouver sites visited, as greater attention was placed on hospitality in a context where people are both socially isolated as well as reluctant to join faith-based communities. Benac notes the importance of what he calls "hubs," where Christians in a variety of models of community (congregations, colleges, arts-based, social action, intentional communities) are gathered, network, and are equipped through a focus on "relations, belonging and possibility within a broader way of life"[68] while resourcing "local leaders to respond adaptively to the challenges they face."[69] Whether established churches or church plants, these Christian initiatives have the potential to engage relationally with six categories as defined by Richard Pitt: transfers, nomads (those moving often from church to church), lapsed former attenders, disillusioned former attenders, the never-churched, and non-believers.[70]

Furthermore, while much of the research, and many of the reflections from pastors and focus group participants, engaged the question of how Christians encounter their non-religious neighbour, there is further reflection needed on how multi-faith presence impacts models of Christian witness. For example, when it came to sharing their faith in public, a couple of focus groups noted how it was easier speaking to people of other world religions than secular Vancouverites. "I had a colleague who was a Confucian and she loved to talk to me about my faith. Another colleague was a Buddhist, and they were always open to faith talk. Those who had no faith expression were less comfortable engaging in conversation." However, another participant noted how when secular Vancouverites were facing difficult times, especially family issues, they were always open when Christians offered to pray for them. "Vancouverites are spiritual in general but hostile towards Christianity in particular," noted one participant. Whether encountering people of no expressed faith belief or those of other world religions, participants noted that pre-existing relationships with neighbours and friends was a key distinctive in sharing the gospel in Vancouver. "Sharing life with neighbours is key, things just come up," said one participant, "In shared life together there is a natural give and take. A neighbour will say, 'Tell me about your Christian beliefs. I'm a Buddhist and I don't know what you believe.'" It was agreed that through friendships and deep relationships, natural conversations take place, and in Vancouver, that includes spaces where people can share their own hurts and disappointments in the experience of the church.

A final thought, since this research began prior to the COVID-19 global pandemic and the fieldwork was conducted during the pandemic, a curiosity remains about the impact of social distancing restrictions and the increased emphasis upon online Christian community (Zoom worship, etc.) and how that may impact Christian communities and the emphasis noted above upon community and belonging. Further research will be needed to explore a further curiosity as to whether the pandemic increased or decreased Vancouver Christians desire for and experience of belonging to a community of faith.

4 GOOD NEWS IN LIGHT OF TROUBLING COLONIAL HISTORY

While Christians seek to share the gospel with their neighbours in Vancouver, the research identified the difficulty of communicating the "good news" of Christianity in light of the "bad news" of colonial mission history, increasingly profiled in the Canadian media. Mission studies scholar Kyo Seong Ahn defines colonialism as "a phenomenon for foreign powers to possess, in many ways forcibly, the land of the indigenous and to rule the indigenous people pursuing their self-interest."[71] Michael Daly notes that "the identification of Christianity with Western culture, and its subsequent evaluation based on the impressions left behind by the colonizers and their missionaries, remains one of the strongest barriers to right relations between Canada's churches and our country's First Nations."[72] Pastors and lay people interviewed in this book consistently named the troubled history of Canadian churches and Indigenous peoples as a stumbling block for sharing the gospel with Vancouverites. As one focus group participant stated, "when I try to share my faith, I usually start off with something light like 'Oh this weekend I'm going to church. Do you go to church?' and people respond, 'No, I hate church.' How do you respond to that?" This person then went on to name the negative depiction of Christianity in the media, especially regarding Residential Schools and treatment of Indigenous peoples and how that hinders Christian witness. It is now well known in Canadian society that throughout the nineteenth and twentieth centuries mainline churches, in partnership with the Canadian government, forcibly removed Indigenous children from their homes and sought to "Westernize" them at the cost of their own culture. In addition, these church-run, government-funded programs subjected many Indigenous children to physical and sexual abuse, with new revelations of the atrocities continuing to surface. Canada's first prime minister Sir John A. Macdonald described the aims of the program in 1887 in this way: "The great aim of our legislation has been to do away with the tribal system and assimilate the Indian people in all respects with other inhabitants of the Dominion as speedily as they are fit to change."[73] Mission scholars Gina Colvin and Rosemary Dewerse note how Christian mission in colonized territories was often understood as "a civilizing mission" of re-enculturation and re-education of Indigenous peoples. Instead, Colvin and Dewerse note that the result of "the spiritual and religious colonization of Indigenous peoples, conducted by Christian empire, inflicted numerous traumas, which, passing from generation to generation, have alienated them from their material, cultural, spiritual, and linguistic resources."[74]

The research clarified how this colonial history is both known by, and impactful upon, the Christian community in Vancouver, especially in light of the church's role in the Residential Schools program.[75] Focus group participants described Residential Schools as "a state-sponsored, church-enforced act of cultural genocide." Both clergy and lay people participating in the research were well informed about how representatives of the church, supported by Indian agents and the Royal Canadian Mounted Police (then the Northwest Mounted Police), seized Indigenous children from their homes, transferred them to church-run boarding schools, and removed, by whatever means necessary, their culture in order to westernize the First Nations.

In 2008, just twelve years after the last residential school in Canada closed, the Truth and Reconciliation Commission of Canada released its report with calls to action for Canadians, including the churches. Canadian theologian Joanne Pepper notes that as the findings of the commission's report became openly available, "socially concerned persons arose as one to query whether Christian missionaries bore culpability for the destabilizing or the euthanizing of indigenous cultures. Disquieted citizens wanted to know: To what degree has Christianity been a mechanism of conflict, injustice and secularizing colonialism in Canada?"[76] Canadian sociologist of religion Sam Reimer describes this challenge for Christians as "incongruity,"[77] whereby there is a clear and public understanding of the gap "between verbalized standards and actual practice,"[78] with the church's participation in Residential Schools program serving as a powerful example of the failure to live out the teachings it espouses (e.g., Matthew 19:13–14). Sociologist of religion Sarah Wilkins-Laflamme highlights the impact of this incongruity on multiple generations of Canadians, noting that "from the 1960s onward, with there being less or no social pressure to be 'a good Christian' to be a 'good Canadian' and with many even associating a number of historical and present social ills with Christianity (such as clergy child sexual abuse scandals as well as the running of Indigenous residential schools in the 19th and 20th centuries), large segments of the Canadian Boomer majority and subsequent generations began and continue today their move away from conventional forms of Christian belonging, belief and ritual."[79]

Even during the researching and writing of this book from 2018–2022, new discoveries were made regarding the church's role in residential schools, with multiple unmarked gravesites of children being discovered on the grounds of former residential school sites across Canada, beginning in Kamloops, British Columbia, in 2020. It was a reminder that the connection between the church and its mission history is a present reality, not a historical footnote. As researcher

Michael Daly asked: "How does a nation begin to speak of reconciliation when confronted with the unreported deaths of more than a
thousand children?"[80] The international media attention on the
church's role in the abuse of Indigenous children made possible an
Indigenous Canadian audience with Pope Francis in Vatican City,
amid calls for the Roman Catholic church to apologize.[81] In turn, this
led to global media attention for a historic visit of Pope Francis to
Canada to meet with Indigenous Peoples and offer a formal apology
for the Roman Catholic Church's treatment of Canada's Indigenous
Peoples.[82] In my interview with Fr Nick Meisl at Holy Rosery
Cathedral, he described some of the challenges for Catholic mission
and engagement in Vancouver from his experience. While the Roman
Catholic Church's position on human sexuality has not changed, he
reflected on the difficulty of offering the gospel to some in the broader
society when they have heard of clergy sexual abuse cases and particularly the discovery of children's graves at church-run residential
schools for Indigenous Canadians. He noted the importance of Pope
Francis's in-person visit to Canada and apology to Indigenous survi-
vors of the residential schools, and the role that will play over time in
restoring confidence in the church in Canada. Fr Meisl observed that
the Catholic church has been slow to respond to these challenges of
abuse and historic wrongs, and that there is not always agreement
within the church leadership on what the right actions might be in
seeking reconciliation. The focus group participants from Holy Rosery
Cathedral also commented at length on the challenge of Christian
witness from a Catholic perspective in Vancouver in light of the media
coverage profiling issues in clergy behaviour and mission history with
Indigenous Canadians.

The research in this book bears evidence of how Christians today
in Vancouver must begin with an awareness that not only is Christianity
an unfamiliar religion to many secular people but also the church is
known by more and more people as an agent of harm rather than a
contributor to the common good. In his research Peter Schuurman,
building on the work of Erving Goffman, notes this challenge for
Christians in Canada coming to terms with their "spoiled identity" in
a post-Christendom Canada whereby they have "a social identity
marked by a perceived undesirable attribute, a shortcoming or failing
that taints them, discounts them, and discredits them if discovered."[83]
In this research, participants from diverse ecclesiastical backgrounds
all identified the challenge of Christian identity in Vancouver in

light of the church's past mission history, with the result at times being their hesitation to engage others in faith conversations. The focus group data illustrated what Schuurman means by "spoiled identity" that "causes constant tension for those in stigmatized environments as they must manage information about themselves or be exposed as lacking credibility."[84]

Added to the history of colonialism and residential schools, the research also identified how contentious the church's previous, and for some Christian initiatives their continuing, opposition to LGBTQI peoples is when it comes to sharing the gospel with non-Christians in Vancouver. This emerged in the conversation with Pastor Sterne of St Peter's Fireside who noted, as a leader within the Anglican Network in Canada, their more traditional understanding of human sexuality can be challenging when trying to connect with the broader, more secular Vancouver culture. He also described the desire of younger members of the church plant to acknowledge and include aspects of reconciliation with Indigenous Peoples (such as a land acknowledgment) in their worship time together. A focus group participant from St Peter's Fireside also noted how a church's viewpoint on social issues, like a more conservative understanding of human sexuality and LGBTQ concerns that St Peter's Fireside holds, makes it difficult to engage more secular people in Vancouver. At nearby St Paul's Anglican Church, focus group members noted how their inclusive LGBTQI position has created space for conversation with their neighbours. Focus group participants described how St Paul's would attend the Pride Parade and then set up a booth at Sunset Beach, offering people "free candles, hugs and prayers" to say publicly and clearly that there are Christians who affirm and love the LGBTQ+ community. It was noted how often volunteers from the church would be in conversations with Pride Parade participants who said it was the first time they had ever been hugged or welcomed by a Christian. The focus group also recalled the church's support for a memorial dedicated to sex workers, paid for by the City of Vancouver, installed on the church grounds, recalling the once ubiquitous sex trade that was part of the neighbourhood until the 1980s.[85] Participants recalled how during the rise of the AIDS epidemic, St Paul's Anglican Church continued the practice of the common cup at Communion, even when many were afraid to be near those suffering from HIV-AIDS. These stories of inclusion seemed to form the key identity of the ministry at St Paul's. However, as I walked along Davie Street with Rev. Cochrane, its businesses adorned with rainbow flags, he acknowledged the challenge of offering a credible Christian witness to the broader LGBTQ+ community that has so often experienced judgment and scorn from the wider Christian community. The negative impression of Christianity in light of its treatment of Indigenous and LGBTQI persons was a recurring theme in this research. Noting this challenging position for the church in the broader society, Canadian missiologist Sam Chaise writes: "something is very different in the current Canadian *zeitgeist*, compared to the one thirty years ago. There is a growing rejection of Christianity. Christianity is not seen as having a positive influence in the Canadian mosaic. The question being asked today is not whether Christianity is true, but whether it is good for Canada and for being human. Increasingly, the answer is 'no.'"[86]

The missional church conversation has long acknowledged the impact of mission history on Christian witness in a post-Christendom landscape. As David Bosch noted, "colonialism and mission, as a matter of course, were interdependent; the right to have colonies carried with it the duty to Christianize the colonized."[87] In the Vancouver context, this legacy has become a significant challenge to the ongoing mission of the church in its attempt to reach out to those who have no church affiliation or background, and whose impression of Christianity is primarily informed through negative media reports of mission history. Here, the research clearly identifies in multiple Christian initiatives both the awareness and desire to engage in meaningful reconciliation with Indigenous Peoples. This will not be a quick process, however, as Philip Sheldrake reminds us: reconciliation requires a complex balance between structural change and spiritual harmony, as well as being evolutionary whereby "long-term and deep reconciliation cannot be achieved without mutual repentance and the discovery of common ground."[88] Focus group participants from Chinese Presbyterian Church expressed deep appreciation for Indigenous culture and noted that Chinese Christians are often perceived to be more trustworthy to Indigenous Peoples because they too have experienced racism and oppression from the colonial powers. "We were discriminated against as well," said one participant, noting the Chinese Head Tax, "and we can share that experience as a bridge with Indigenous Peoples." This observation echoes Wesley Granberg-Michaelson's own observations on the interconnectedness between Indigenous and non-Western immigrant Christianity in congregational studies in the United States where he argues that "for Christians of all theological persuasions formed by modern Western culture, an imperative of our journey is learning to see reality through non-Western eyes." He continues: "Critiques of modern secularism provide helpful insight, but the lived experience of Native American communities, as well as the diverse non-Western cultures in Africa and Asia, with creative expressions of Christian faith within those contexts, all can serve to teach and enrich us."[89]

The research presented in this book bears evidence that the work of reconciliation between Christian initiatives and those harmed by the church's mission past has begun in earnest in Vancouver. At Jacob's Well in the Downtown Eastside neighbourhood it was noted in interviews that the church's history with Indigenous Peoples makes it difficult sometimes to engage others in faith talk, especially if they have been hurt by the church. One participant described how the prayer room in the ministry last year went through a season where it was almost all Indigenous Christian art. One day when they were praying, several Indigenous people came in from the street and lay down on the ground to sleep in the prayer room. The Indigenous men later said that they felt safe in the space because they recognized the art and felt at home. Creating space with Indigenous art and language is becoming more common in Christian settings in Vancouver, with many of the initiatives studied including an Indigenous land acknowledgment in their time of worship and introducing themes of reconciliation with Indigenous Peoples in their preaching and print materials. Many focus group participants articulated the desire to build closer relationships with Indigenous Peoples but also a corresponding lack of understanding in how to take those steps forward. As one focus group participant said, "we have been created as Chinese, Scottish, Indigenous, etc. and we are all equally loved by God – his children loved equally. And so, we need to care for one another in like fashion – it's a starting place for mission." This respect for Indigenous Peoples, and the desire for Christians to address past colonial wrongs while building positive relationships moving forward, was present in all the initiatives studied in the fieldwork. That is worth noting given the wide ecumenical scope of the research. In addition, it is important to acknowledge that this is not an activity originating and moving in one direction alone, from "settler Canadians" to Indigenous Peoples. It is noteworthy that a large percentage of Indigenous people in Canada self-identify as Christian, despite the legacy of colonialism and residential schools. As former Indigenous Anglican Church of Canada Archbishop Mark

MacDonald notes, this reality is a miracle and offers evidence in Canada of the emergence of "a distinctly indigenous Christian faith and its post-Christendom flowering in our time."[90] Participants in the research clearly and consistently displayed an openness (even an eagerness) to learn from Indigenous spirituality and understand the integration of traditional beliefs with Christian thought. This positive turn towards Indigenous identity and spirituality is a significant finding in the research, given Christianity's historic repression of First Nation's culture. This included the Canadian government's outlawing of the Potlatch ceremony from 1884 to 1951, that impacted traditional Indigenous communities including the role of women, as well as Christian missionaries deeming totem poles and other cultural practices as "sinful" and "pagan."[91] Cascadian-based Indigenous missiologist Randy Woodley notes the theological importance of non-Indigenous Christians embrace of First Nations' spirituality for the sake of decolonized church. Woodley writes that "characteristics of Indigenous theology and practice have a creation-based theological foundation that emphasizes harmony and balance, being centred and seeking cooperation" with a worldview that is "physically and morally holistic, a very tangible spirituality, egalitarian, peace seeking, cooperative, purposeful and meaningful work, a natural interconnectedness to all creation, hospitality, and generosity."[92] Clearly, based on the findings of this book and with a growing interest in church and academia, this question of what Indigenous Christianity means for Christian witness in Vancouver is an area for further research.

5 THE CHANGING FACE OF CHRISTIANITY IN VANCOUVER

Rooted in the familiar secularization thesis, many have assumed that Christianity is in steep decline in Vancouver since many of those with European Christendom heritage have ended any formal association with organized religion, from regular churchgoing to rites of passage such as Christian baptisms, weddings, and funerals. For these Vancouverites, when they (or their parents) moved to the West Coast, the newcomers left behind whatever Christian faith they may have once practised. Scholars such as Oliver Roy are blunter in their assessment of the current state of the secular West: "A common drawback today is that lay culture has forgotten its religious roots. This is not a result of anti-clericalism or a militant anti-religious stance: it is ignorance."[93]

This was clear in the fieldwork where many participants described their neighbours or co-workers' reaction to Christian faith in terms of apathy. One respondent wrote in a follow-up email after the focus group interview: "Most people I know say, 'Oh, you go to church? I think maybe my grandparents did that. That's cool.' And then they tell me that they are off to cycle Stanley Park on Sunday or go skiing up Grouse Mountain without any interest or sense that my Christian faith might have something important to offer their lives."[94] Here we see evidence of Hugh McLeod's observation that "the decline of Christendom has meant that Christianity has been gradually losing its status as a lingua franca, and has tended to become a local language used by those who are professing Christians."[95] This was summarized in a focus group participant's comment that "most Vancouverites do not really understand what Christianity is really about and why we do what we do for Jesus. It isn't a judgmental approach, rather it is more apathetic in that classic Vancouver 'you do you' approach to life."

But the research also suggests there is another story to be told. As Claire Dwyer observed, "the city of Vancouver may be a less well-known example of a global city, but it is characteristic of a range of emerging global cities, particularly orientated towards Asian trans-national circuits of capital and migration."[96] In building an urban missiology of Vancouver on the Pacific Rim, missiologists would do well to look in the direction of Asia rather than Europe since the Christian community in Vancouver today is increasingly marked by the presence of Asian believers rather than those with European heritage. Further study of the secularizing impact of the Vancouver culture on the 1.5 and 2.0 generations of these Asian immigrants is needed. For example, recent research has named the "in-between" status of Asian immigrant believers as "Jook-sing" – a Cantonese term for an overseas-born Chinese person.[97] "Jook-sing" is the stem of a bamboo plant that does not allow water to flow out the other end, thus metaphorically "Jook-sing Christians" have flowed from Asia to Canada but struggle to exit into the mainstream Canadian society, feeling caught between two worlds, including in the church. Understanding the struggle of new Canadians who identify as Christian will be essential for churches in Vancouver, including those in this study, which were all experiencing the impact of immigration in their ministries. Fr Nick Meisl at Holy Rosary Cathedral observed that "the first thing you need to know is that without the overwhelming immigration of faithful Catholics from the Philippines we would be in trouble."

He noted that while there are a few ethnic-specific parishes in the archdiocese from Korean churches in Surrey and Port Moody to Mandarin-speaking parishes in Richmond, the impact of Filipino immigration has impacted almost every parish across the diocese. For example, Fr Meisl noted that at the cathedral when he stands each week to say Mass and looks out at the congregation, most of the worshippers are Filipinos. He mentioned that in his experience the 1.0, 1.5, and 2.0 generations of Filipino Catholic immigrants appear to be staying active in the local parishes, unlike so many immigrant groups where the second generation begins to drift from the church.

In a number of the field sites and focus groups engaged, there appears to be much vibrancy in the ethnic-specific congregations (e.g., Chinese Presbyterian, Pacific Grace Mennonite Brethren) and in large pan-Asian multi-site churches (e.g., Tenth Kits, Tapestry–Marpole), with a growing Asian Christian presence in established churches (e.g., Oakridge United, First Christian Reformed) and in the Roman Catholic Archdiocese (with immigration profoundly impacting the Orthodox church as well). Indeed, in reviewing the data from this research, Angus Reid,[98] a renowned Vancouver-based sociologist and Canadian pollster, identified the ethnic diversity present as noteworthy and essential for understanding what Christianity looks like on the West Coast today. Reid wrote: "I was quite impressed with the number of recent immigrants and first-generation Canadians included. I think this is an important matter that deserves further analysis."[99] Another prominent Canadian sociologist, Sam Reimer, identifies the importance of immigration on the Canadian church in his recent study noting, "in Canada, the vast majority of future growth (religious or otherwise) will likely depend on immigration ... with these immigrants have come new denominations and religious networks. These groups are typically charismatic/Pentecostal, and they will grow as traditional evangelical churches decline."[100]

The focus group discussions offered evidence that Vancouver Christians from a non-European heritage felt they had an advantage in sharing the gospel with their non-Christian neighbours, including Indigenous Peoples. Many of those interviewed identified that they moved to Vancouver from places where Christianity is a minority or persecuted expression (e.g., China or Indonesia) and described this as an advantage in engaging in Christian witness and mission. Canadian sociologists of religion such as Joel Thiessen are beginning to take note of this shift. He writes: "Truth be told, levels of individual secularization would likely be worse if it were not for immigration. Immigration keeps Christian identification, belief, and practice afloat, notably in Roman Catholic and conservative Protestant settings."[101]

Furthermore, a shadow side of this reality to be explored in future research is the identification of racism towards this growing non-European Christian population both inside the church and in the wider community. For example, church leaders such as Rev. Victor Kim, who served at Richmond Presbyterian Church, led public rallies against anti-Asian flyers distributed in the community by members of the alt-right.[102] Pastor Ken Shigematsu at Tenth Church has described the racism he faced arriving as the church's first Asian pastor twenty years ago, but how that experience shaped his leadership of a thriving multi-site church, now focused on inclusion and welcome, including being among the first in the Alliance tradition with female elders and a notable LGBTQI presence in the congregation. Drawing on his own experiences of exclusion as an Asian male Christian leader, Pastor Shigematsu remarked on the presence of those normally excluded in evangelical churches, such as female leaders and LGBTQI: "They feel the resonance of truth here. The welcome of community, the spiritual vitality. They discern the presence of God." At the other end of the spectrum, "if social justice is devoid of the beauty and power of Christ, it can still be a valuable thing, but not as unique as it is when the Holy Spirit illumines who Jesus is."[103]

As the research discovered, however, congregations reflecting these changing demographics bring their own congregational cultures and challenges. Pastor Bill Chan reflected that Chinese ministries are a bit like "Grandpa's house." Grandpa built the house (1.0 generation Cantonese or Mandarin) and now is happy to have his children (1.5 hybrid) or grandchildren (2.0 English ministry) visit, but it is still Grandpa's house. Change is not welcome in a way that other non-ethnic-specific ministries may not experience. "That's why," Pastor Chan suggested, "people who come to pastor from outside often miss the bicultural dimensions of the power here. You may be pastoring the English ministry, but you must have respect and appreciation for the Cantonese or Mandarin ministries that started this place." Pastor Chan reflected that his congregation is primarily a commuter church from all over Vancouver, but that when it comes to mission, people in his English ministry congregation are keen to engage the neighbourhood and use the building for outreach, compared to the Cantonese or Mandarin congregations under the same roof who hold the balance of power in the leadership. "Don't mess up Grandpa's house," Pastor Chan said with a smile, "Keep it tidy."

This research has problematized the assumption that the church in Vancouver is in clear (and seemingly inevitable) decline. We have raised the question of whether the church in Vancouver is perhaps *changing*, alongside the traditional narratives of the church declining or disappearing. To be clear, the number of Canadians self-identifying as Christian is declining in significant numbers according to the latest census data from Statistics Canada, and denominations report declining membership and churches closing across the country, with the United Church of Canada alone reporting a 40 per cent drop in membership.[104] To suggest that the church in Vancouver is changing *as well as* declining is not to deny the real challenge of church decline. Rather, this research invites the reader to look closer to see where the life and energy is coming from in the Christian church in this region, amidst an overall decline in those who self-identify as Christian. Throughout this research, we have been clear that statistically Christians are a minority within the city of Vancouver. However, this research invites us to attend to divine presence in those places that "fly under the radar," including ethnic-specific churches, or to the growing numbers of Asian believers in all churches in Vancouver that will be an important research field requiring further study. Here, we note the prophetic description of mission by the late Cascadian-born, Chicago-based urban missiologist Ray Bakke: "Mission is no longer about crossing the oceans, jungles, and deserts, but about crossing the streets of the world's cities. From now on, nearly all ministry will be cross-cultural amid the urban pluralism caused by the greatest migration in human history."[105] Forecasting the future, Canadian sociologist of religion Reginald Bibby declared that "there is no single factor that is going to be more important in determining the future of life in Canada than immigration."[106] While the changing face of Christianity (with a significant Asian influence) has been identified in this research, it will be important to have follow-up research exploring this impact upon Christian initiatives in Vancouver over the next decade.

6 SCARCE SACRED SPACE

A significant finding in this study is that a particular challenge for Christian communities in Vancouver is finding and maintaining ecclesiastical meeting and service space. For example, Rev. Heather Joy James at Oakridge United Church noted with regret how difficult it is for many Christian communities to find worship space to rent in Vancouver, and yet one of the things that mainline Protestant churches still have to offer is physical property for Christian mission. However, redevelopment of these properties is challenging in the current Vancouver context. Rev. Joy James offered a series of examples of congregations in the city that ran into trouble with issues as wide ranging as city zoning policy, unsavoury developers, or a facility that in the end was not particularly suitable for the church's mission.[107]

Pastor Matheson of Tenth Kits shared his frustration with finding suitable space to meet for worship and lamented the loss of the Anglican Church of Canada site they once used and how well suited it was for their congregation. The church sanctuary, kitchen, and meeting rooms were spacious; the location had great visibility in the neighbourhood; and parking was plentiful. The Anglican Church space was sold, however, to a developer for luxury condos just before the pandemic and Tenth Kits had to move again. Pastor Matheson reflected on the disappointment he and the congregation felt when the Anglican Archdiocese would not negotiate with them for purchase of the building, choosing instead to go for the more lucrative offer from a developer. "Once ecclesiastical space is gone in Vancouver these days, it's gone for good," he said with a hint of frustration. Moving entirely online for the pandemic, the congregation shared their worship with the other Tenth Church sites and had only recently returned to meeting in-person. Now they are renting space in the nearby Museum of Vancouver. "It's a good space for worship," Pastor Matheson reflected, "and is giving us flexibility to try new ways of worshipping together, including moving chairs around for discussion after the sermon." He noted that it also provides rooms for the children and youth to meet separately, and joked, "there are only a few Museum goers on a Sunday morning who stumble into our worship." Pastor Matheson shared, however, that just as they were getting familiar with their new location at the Museum of Vancouver, they received word of a major renovation of the space that would require them to move out in a few months. He once again lamented the lack of ecclesiastical space in Vancouver. All this change comes in the midst of the uncertainty of what church will be like post-pandemic. "We lose people every time we change sites. It's inevitable," Pastor Matheson said, "But now, it's especially difficult as we try to figure out who is coming back and who has gone somewhere else." Kits Tenth highlights again the common story of churches in Vancouver struggling to find, maintain, or repurpose ecclesiastical space. Vancouver is not alone in this challenge, as demonstrated in other research on church plants by Christopher James in Seattle and Richard Pitt in a wider study of twelve American cities.[108]

Given that Vancouver is home to some of the most expensive real estate in the world,[109] the fieldwork highlighted the dilemma of faithful stewardship of property for those churches that are fortunate to have buildings, and the ongoing challenge of immigrant churches and church plants that are new to the city and cannot find a place to gather for worship and service. Between 2009 and 2018, Canada lost 17 per cent of its churches, with Canada Revenue Agency and Charities Directorate reporting that British Columbia lost 443 churches in that period.[110] As Canadian church planter Kevin Makins noted of Canada's largest cities, "the Canadian Broadcasting Company has said that Canada is on track to close over nine thousand sacred buildings in the next decade, roughly one-third of all our religious spaces."[111] As noted in chapter 3 with Oakridge United Church, the redevelopment of an older church building into housing with a smaller worship space left church members describing the need for a visible presence of the church in the community. One focus group participant from Oakridge United Church noted the importance of being physically present in the community as a sign of Christian witness: "I think our mission is opening the door literally, keeping the door propped open to the wider community. People can hear what is going on. People do come in and check us out. They might not come back, but they know we're open to the community and that we're not a private club." In what Philip Sheldrake calls "sacramentality" – a material sign of God's action in human lives – the question remains about the visibility of the Christian community, at least in the form of ecclesiastical buildings, when one of the major challenges to life in Vancouver is affordable real estate.[112] While medieval cathedrals are considered "texts" in the broad sense implied by semiotics, what do we say about the Christian witness of architecturally unremarkable post-war ecclesiastical edifices now in need of either repair or redevelopment? Are these older, often poorly maintained buildings seen by the broader secular community as a witness or simply a development opportunity?[113]

David Garbin and Anna Strhan muse about what the impact might be of urban restrictions on religious communities when they write, "struggles over the meaning and use of everyday urban space are of

major significance in reaffirming or contesting the dominant production of space. While, apart from a few notable exceptions, the question
of religious and sacred space has generally been absent from ... recent
literature on urban social movements."[114] This is certainly true in
Vancouver where the issue of diminishing sacred space has not been
widely addressed in the media or academia. In recent years, denominational efforts at redevelopment have been formed – such as the
United Church of Canada's new real estate body and ecumenical
organizations such as the Trinity Centres Foundation repurposing
ecclesiastical space for broader community use – to try to address this
challenge of a declining number of church buildings in Canada.[115]

Of course, this concern regarding the decline of sacred space in
Vancouver is not one that we should necessarily assume alarms the
general, more secular public. Nor should we assume it troubles civic
politicians who would often prefer to rezone a religious assembly
space (that currently brings in zero property tax to city hall due to
Christendom-era exemptions) and create zoning to provide for-profit,
taxable housing or commercial space. As Canadian sociologist Joel
Thiessen notes, the demand for religion is not as strong in Canada as
once thought, and no matter how relevant the preaching, lively the
music, effective the programming, or caring an environment offered,
the data from his study determined that "the reasons for diminished
involvement and the potential reasons for greater involvement are
largely beyond what religious groups can control."[116] He notes that
having no religious identity is now more culturally acceptable in
Canada,[117] combined with a significant increase in Canadian teens
moving into adulthood with no religious affiliation and fewer non-
religious adults marrying religiously active partners.[118] This means
that there is a dwindling pool of active participants in Christian initiatives or those on the margins with a potential to be reactivated in
religious practice. So, are there others in the wider Vancouver landscape who share the concern of Christians regarding the continuing
presence of sacred space in physical buildings, when so many secular
Vancouverites choose instead to gather in natural outdoor gathering
places such as parks? If not, that suggests a difficult road ahead for
the older established European-heritage denominations that once
sought to build something like a Christendom presence in Vancouver
and now hold valuable, but aging and costly infrastructure. However,
as we noted early in this chapter, the changing face of Christianity in
Vancouver, and its corresponding influence, may have an impact that

is yet hard to forecast as members of these new communities exert their public voice, economic resources, and political connections.

There remains an unexplored area of research regarding ecclesiastical space, specifically whether the high cost of real estate and limited zoning for religious public assembly left available will not only bring about greater ecumenical co-operation but also perhaps multi-faith sharing of space. That Canada today is a pluralistic or "multiple mosaic society" with a strong emphasis on equality, justice, and social compassion is, according to sociologist of religion Reginald Bibby, the fruit of the multiculturalism policy first enacted in the 1970s by the Liberal government under Prime Minister Pierre Trudeau and a tremendous challenge for historic Euro-tribal denominations. Bibby argues that the multicultural infant has grown up, left home, and touched virtually all of life. Today in Canada, we have not only a cultural mosaic but also a value mosaic, a leisure mosaic, a concern mosaic, a sexual mosaic, a gender mosaic, a family mosaic, a religion mosaic, and so on.[119] This mosaic reality may make for some interesting partnerships in future years as religious groups of various backgrounds seek public assembly space in an increasing expensive and secular Vancouver context.

7 ECOLOGY AND THEOLOGY

As noted throughout this study, Vancouverites place a high social value on both the care for and enjoyment of the physical environment. Some commentators on religion in the city, such as *Vancouver Sun* newspaper columnist Douglas Todd, have even gone so far as to call environmentalism Vancouver's commonly held "civic religion" or what Philip Sheldrake calls "the soul of the city."[120] From Vancouver as the birthplace of the environmental activist organization Greenpeace to the stunning beauty of oceans and mountains captured by the tourist board's slogan "Super, Natural British Columbia" to the limitless outdoor recreation opportunities, this research demonstrates that Vancouver's engagement with the environment is something that Christians must take seriously when considering mission in the city.

The focus groups in this study explored questions of how Vancouverite's reverence for the environment could present both challenge and opportunity for Christians in sharing a soteriological message based on Jesus. One participant observed that "our way forward is to have a missional theology embraced by all the churches in Vancouver that is incarnational and holistic in its understanding of the gospel. If that could seep into the church across Vancouver, then we would see creation care and Indigenous culture more naturally addressed and embraced." In following up on this understanding of "incarnational and holistic," the participant noted that too often Christianity is seen as something that takes place within a building, rather than connecting with God and others in the beauty of creation. Focus group participants identified several values common to Vancouverites, including an emphasis on the natural environment and being outdoors while engaging in physical fitness. One participant noted that "there is a common desire to be 'green' and reduce our carbon footprint. This translates on the local level in Vancouver to shared, urban gardening, the preference by many for public transit or electric vehicles, composting and recycling, and a civic pride in public space such as parks (including Stanley Park), beaches, and hiking in the North Shore Mountains."

Social justice was also named by participants as a shared value by Vancouverites, with a propensity for social activism and public demonstrations of protest, including old-growth forest logging blockades and Extinction Rebellion[121] sit-ins that shut down traffic. Respect for Indigenous issues was another commonly held value named by all participants with examples of the widespread practice in Vancouver of a land acknowledgment. One participant said that "Indigenous issues are public now, with land acknowledgments heard everywhere, from a Vancouver Canucks game to the local casino."

The desire to actively engage in the world from a faith perspective was echoed by many of the Christian initiatives interviewed, including Jacob's Well ministries. Its mission statement says, in part: "We believe our common purpose as followers of Christ is to announce the good news (Gospel) of the Kingdom of God, a Kingdom of justice and shalom, where nothing is missing or broken, where all things are reconciled and restored. We do this in word and action, longing and working for right relationships between God, ourselves, our fellow humans, and creation." Those interviewed for this book consistently expressed that a faithful desire to care for creation was tied to action. As one focus group participant said, "talk is cheap. Action matters. How can we reduce our carbon footprint and where are the Christian organizations, like A Rocha, making a difference? What would it look like to have the whole church take a day and have a collective cleanup of the neighbourhood?" Participants pointed to community gardens (First Christian Reformed Church, Kitsilano Christian Community) as examples of churches connecting with the environment and their neighbourhoods.

As well, the biblical theme of Sabbath was named as an example of living as a countercultural witness, demonstrating that Christians in Vancouver can live differently amongst neighbours without buying into the dominant capitalistic model in the world. Some of the Christian initiatives expressly link creation with soteriology, such as the downtown church plant St Peter's Fireside, an Anglican Network in Canada parish, with a traditional understanding of human sexuality that seeks to reach urban professionals. In the fieldwork, I noted that part of their doctrinal statement includes the following: "Jesus came into the world to seek and save all that is lost, to die to forgive us for all our sins and reconcile us to God, and to save us from everything that tarnishes, pollutes, and distorts us and God's good creation." St Paul's Anglican Church, an Anglican Church of Canada parish with a pro-inclusion approach to human sexuality, also names the importance of creation care with the ministry of Jesus. St Paul's website states: "We believe that God is calling us to greater diversity of membership (to better reflect the neighbourhoods we serve), wider participation in mission, ministry and leadership, better stewardship in God's creation and a stronger resolve in challenging attitudes and structures that cause injustice."[122]

The link between belief in Jesus and creation was evident through participant observation of the worship life of initiatives, including in the sermons. For example, in my site visit to Oakridge United Church, Rev. Joy James encouraged worshippers to feel an interconnectedness with one another and all creation through "our friend Jesus." Focus group participants at Oakridge United Church noted that "Vancouverites value the environment, they have a common love of the outdoors, being close to the ocean and spending time in Stanley Park or up in the North Shore mountains. Of course, it is an 'urban wilderness' where you are always close to the city and its amenities."

Creation care was also highlighted by focus group participants at Tenth Kits, with many commenting on the frequency during preaching of care for creation being named as a discipleship task. Concern for creation and attention to its missional implications for Christian witness in Vancouver was evident in the ethnically specific congregations as well. Focus group participants from Pacific Grace MB Church said enthusiastically that "the environment is easy to connect with here in

Vancouver – creation care is so important to believers and non-believers. We're stewards of God's creation, and we've been entrusted to care for it." Reflecting on what that means for connecting missionally with others, someone said: "So, our goal is the same with non-Christians and here is where our commonality comes from, the opportunity to both share the gospel and ask where does your hope for this world come from? They may or may not have an origin story of why they care about the environment, but it is a shared value and an opportunity to share faith." At St Paul's Anglican Church participants also made this connection between creation and witness noting that "the church needs to find a way of saying *why we care* about things like recycling, to speak about God's love and God's creation as our motivating factors for involvement."

Indeed, Philip Sheldrake names "ecology" as one of the key values of "the good city," noting "that is to say (the good city) minimizes the ecological footprint, balances nature with the built environment and encourages efficient building."[123] The research demonstrated, however, that for Christians living in Vancouver this attention to creation care meant more than being a good citizen and recycling when possible. It was a reminder that Christians have a rich and storied engagement regarding a theology of creation, and that Christian communities can be places where this love of God's world is made known from leafy green neighbourhoods to the hardscrabble reality of the Downtown Eastside. For example, participants at Jacob's Well sought to show a different side of their often-stereotyped neighbourhood that is not known for its natural beauty. One participant said that "care for the environment here means looking out for trash on the streets, watching for signs of beauty like a flower growing up through the cracks of the pavement." Here we see evidence of Christopher James's Neighborhood Incarnation model, where participants understand their parish as "places of beauty, need and hope."[124] In addition, being able to articulate and embody a different understanding of the world around them as "creation" rather than "nature" becomes an essential witness for Vancouver Christians and provides both a corrective and a bridge for partnership with their more secular neighbours, who care for the environment and reject the historic extraction approach of British Columbia's mining and forestry industries.

The focus on ecology and theology that emerged from the data has been identified by others in Vancouver over the years. For example, Jonathan Wilson laments the "far-reaching and damaging effects of the loss of teleology" in what he describes as "the transformation of creation into nature."[125] As a Vancouver theologian, Wilson argues this turn to nature is the conviction that the world is all that there ever has been and ever will be. Echoing Canadian philosopher Charles Taylor in *A Secular Age*, Wilson notes that even Christians in this "immanent frame" are conditioned to see the world around them within the self-governing norms of nature. What I have identified elsewhere as "Christian Functional Atheism,"[126] Wilson describes in this way: "people are most often 'practical naturalists,' confessing belief in God and creation and afterlife while living as if this world were all there ever has been and ever will be."[127] While people may not feel a bond to each other as closely here in Vancouver as neighbours might to each other "back east" in the rest of Canada, there *is* a close bond with nature and human beings' responsible care for it.[128] Mark Shibley concurs, arguing that "much contemporary environmentalism in the Northwest is a religious system, not simply because it is sometimes dogmatic and moralistic but rather because its rituals and core beliefs distinguish between things sacred (wilderness) and things profane (all else, often including people)."[129] University of Victoria scholar Paul Bramadat suggests calling the deeply held value of the environment in the region "reverential naturalism" and describes it as the metanarrative of the Pacific Northwest. Bramadat defines reverential naturalism as "a broad and naturalized schema that helps to explain the ways Cascadians think and talk about religion, spirituality, and nature" that "favours an orientation that is both accepting of scientific approaches to nature and inclined to perceive and imagine the natural world in ways that are redolent of mysticism, panentheism, animism, pantheism, and inclusive forms of theism."[130]

Therefore, what is clear from the research is that Vancouver Christians are both aware of the high value that their non-Christian (and likely secular) neighbours place on the environment, as well as mindful of their opportunity to articulate a Christian theology of creation as a powerful narrative for shaping a response to the crisis of climate change. To engage in mission in Vancouver today without this sensitivity to the environment would be futile. Stefan Paas notes this importance of attending to environmental issues for urban Christians in the West by asking, "and how could churches evangelize credibly in the secular, post-Christian city without being involved in justice and environmental issues?"[131] Seeking this overlapping consensus with non-Christian neighbours in care for the planet remains a viable mission approach for Christians in Vancouver. As Paul Williams, professor at Vancouver's Regent College writes, "the hopes of the environmental movement for conservativism, sustainable living, and democratic participation are hopes that Christians can affirm enthusiastically."[132]

Having explored these seven significant observations emerging from the research into Christianity in Vancouver, we now turn to our final chapter and tentatively offer proposals for the wider question of urban witness through a missional lens for North America.

5

The Next Faithful Step

Towards an Urban Missiology for Vancouver

Chapter 1 identified the aim of this monograph to provide thick(er) descriptions of Christian initiatives' missional interaction in Canada's largest Pacific Rim city. While a surprising number of North American missional church leaders have lived experience in Vancouver, including Alan Roxburgh, Ross Hastings, Michael Goheen, and Scott Hagley, these consultants and academics have written primarily about the missional church in general across North America, without particular emphasis on the city of Vancouver beyond the anecdotal. As both a congregational minister and academic living in Vancouver, I was curious (based on a conviction of the *missio Dei*) to explore in a fulsome way what God was up to here on the West Coast. Long known for its secular and liberal culture, Vancouver appeared to be a potential "ecclesiastical Petri dish" where study of the church in this context might provide clues for Christian witness in other Canadian cities as they moved further into post-Christendom. Therefore, I designed an ethnographic/urban research project in the field of congregational studies, without limiting the research to congregations alone. The research employed in this book made use of qualitative methods including observation, analyzing texts and documents, interviewing, recording, and transcription.[1]

Throughout the research and writing for this book I did not pretend to play the role of the detached observer but rather, as a resident of Vancouver, engaging the world through a confessional lens as a Reformed Christian, I brought almost two decades of experience in the city to bear on the work, acknowledging the potential value of a personal perspective. I was curious to know more about the diverse ways that Christians were gathering in the city, reflected now in the data from the fourteen field sites that kindly gave so much of their time and informed perspectives to this work. The research led me to wonder further about how the Christian community perceived the wider culture of Vancouver, as well as how they were responding to fellow Vancouverites in order to live, share, and show the gospel. Reflecting on the data generated, I also wondered what lessons this book might have to offer to the wider, and ongoing, missiological discussion in Canada as we seek to build thick(er) descriptions by answering the question, "How are Christians in Vancouver today, as a minority expression of the majority secular population, organizing their communities, shaping their beliefs, and expressing themselves in mission?" A thick description seeks to "capture the essence of a phenomenon in a way that communicates it" in a more fulsome way.[2] In the process of developing and describing this thick description of missional interaction with the city of Vancouver, I have felt one part adventurer, learning new things about the community I proudly call home, and another part docent, leading the reader through familiar ecclesiastical and civic territory that I have experienced in my leadership roles in church and academia here for nearly two decades.

This final chapter attempts to answer the question set out at the beginning of this research journey, placing those provisional findings in conversation with the ongoing missional theology conversation (with a particular emphasis upon the Canadian context) in order to make a humble yet helpful contribution to both church and academia.

THEOLOGICAL FRAMEWORK OF EXILE

Over the last several decades, the theme of exile has become popular within the missional theology discourse in North America to describe the shift from late-stage Christendom to early post-Christendom.[3] Old Testament scholar Walter Brueggemann is perhaps best known in North America for providing early theological reflection on the theme of exile and how it describes the experience of the church's movement from the centre of power to the margins.[4] Others have used the theme of exile as a way of describing the experience of no longer being at home in the wider culture, including Will Willimon and Stanley Hauerwas's work *Resident Aliens*. Indeed, using the lens of exile to help understand God's agency at work amidst a season of disruption can be a helpful aid for Christians today trying to make sense of their place in a post-Christian society. As Stefan Paas notes, "to adopt the narratives of exile and diaspora as a hermeneutical lens to contexts of deep secularization suggests that secularization may be part of God's mission after all."[5] Recently, however, some in the Canadian missional theology conversation have pushed back against the now-familiar framework of exile to describe the experience of Christians in a post-Christendom context. Vancouver-based missiologist Alan Roxburgh challenges the assumption that exile is the right lens for describing our current reality by arguing that "while psychologically appealing, exile has no material relationship to the situation of the Euro-tribal churches. The people of these churches are members of the dominant cultures. They are, overall, middle-class, white-collar, and have been very well situated inside the sociocultural reality of the globalized West. Their members run corporations, sit on town and city councils, run businesses, and teach in schools. The metaphor appeals to the experiences of unraveling ... the problem is that the people of the Euro-tribal churches haven't been sent anywhere against their will and are not dwelling in some strange land. Many other things may be happening, but this metaphor does not describe their reality."[6] Roxburgh advances the argument that Christians in Canada have not been removed to a foreign land, rather they have remained in place, passively watching the culture change around them without making necessary missional changes along the way. Roxburgh's critique of exile makes Canadian Christians sound more like those left in Jerusalem after 586 BCE rather than the people taken to Babylon, even though one could argue those left behind experienced deep trauma as well. In addition, we identified earlier in this book the growing scholarly consensus led by Lynn Marks and Tina Block that Christendom was never fully established in Vancouver, thus making it more challenging to apply some of the wider missional literature's assumptions about the end of Christendom on Christian witness here. If the Church in Vancouver was never a Christendom expression of ecclesiology, how do you mourn the loss of something you never had? Of course, Roxburgh, Marks, and Block's arguments must be read with an awareness that exile is not just a sociological category. Rather, it is a heuristic category that may apply more or less depending on the context, with the intention of bringing out perspectives that would otherwise have gone unnoticed. Nevertheless, the theological framework of exile helps name the church's profound dislocation from power today (whether it was fully vested as in eastern Canada or lightly felt as in British Columbia). Stefan Paas argues that the exile traditions from the Old Testament "shed new light on the 'disembedding' of Christianity from our societies," noting that exile is a time of confusion; exile is characterized by a loss of power; it requires looking after one's own identity; and exile asks for a renewed spirituality.[7] The Vancouver churches profiled in this research were self-aware of the marginal role of Christianity in public spaces, as well as the challenge of living their faith within a broader culture that often view Christianity with a mix of apathy and suspicion. Whether Vancouver Christians identify with exiles in Babylon, those who remained in the rubble of Jerusalem, or others who moved further afield in the diaspora, the impact of the disorientating forces of exile still resonate as a theological framework for Vancouver Christians today.

OUTCOMES FROM THE RESEARCH

As we near the end of our journey, we turn now to the larger curiosity about what God is up to in Vancouver in light of the data generated and how this learning might impact both local church leaders and contribute to the larger missional church conversation in North America. While these findings are more speculative than conclusive, the hope is that the following five proposals, building out from the seven observations in the last chapter, will resonate with those leading Christian initiatives in Vancouver as well as advance the ongoing reflections and discourse on mission in academia today.

1 Mission through Relationships

The research in this book, representing a diversity of denominations, theological perspectives, and neighbourhoods, offers consistent and clear evidence that Christians in Vancouver are placing a high value on the building of relationships with their non-Christian neighbours in order to share and show the gospel. To be clear, this is not part of a wider evangelistic program such as "friendship evangelism," which tends to treat one's neighbour as object rather than subject. There was data that Christians recognized both the deep isolation and loneliness in their neighbours as well as the gospel's call to love their neighbour as a way of engaging in witness. Christian leaders in Vancouver would be wise to note that traditional evangelistic techniques such as revivalist gatherings and street preaching did not resonate with Christians in this research.

What became clear from studying the data is that Christian initiatives in Vancouver need to build deep relational connections with their non-Christian neighbours in order to create space, over a period of time, to share and show the gospel. Christian witness detached from relationship appears to be ineffective and unhelpful in the highly secularized and diverse Vancouver context. Here, the Vancouver research resonates with the study on evangelism by Alpha Canada in 2021 that found "the most encouraged and practiced method of evangelization today is showing vs. telling" with 45 per cent of churches reporting that they encourage their members to show one's faith through their actions.[8] Researchers noted that relationships create opportunities for sharing faith through actions, inviting a person to church, showing hospitality, and talking about faith, with the number one reason a person joins a faith group being because a trusted friend or family member has extended an invitation to them.[9] Set within the theological framework of exile, the outcome of mission through relationships resonates with Jeremiah 29:7, "Also, seek the peace and prosperity of the city to which I have carried you into exile." This commitment by Vancouver Christians to build deep and meaningful relationships with their non-Christian neighbours appears to be rooted in an outward turning of the church to the city and its inhabitants in order to seek and increase God's shalom for all. Some may think this is simply an act of "Canadian niceness or politeness," and in the Canadian context the wider culture does exert some pressure against more public confrontational prophetic action. Canadian sociologist Sam Reimer has named this characteristic "irenicism" when profiling the differences between Canadian and American evangelicals who share a similar subculture. By irenicism, Reimer means "attitudes towards other individuals or groups that are not sectarian, partisan, prejudiced, or patriarchal."[10] Those participating in the research were able to connect their engagement of non-Christian neighbours (without traditional proselytizing) with a deep desire to love their neighbour and to discern opportunities to share and show their Christian faith at the same time. Sam Reimer has named this respectful restraint in Canadian evangelicals as "civility," by which he means a "tendency to communicate in a polite and noncombative way ... also a part of irenicism as I define it."[11] If there is a biblical verse beyond the exile narrative to connect with this outcome of the research it could be 1 Peter 3:15, "But in your hearts revere Christ as Lord. Always be prepared to give an answer to everyone who asks you to give the reason for the hope that you have. But do this with gentleness and respect." A challenge and opportunity emerging from this outcome for Christian leaders in Vancouver is to ask, "How are churches equipping their members for their relational engagement with non-Christians when they are not gathered on a Sunday morning?"

2 Mission through Creation Care

Throughout the research for this book a shared value identified in both the Christian community and the wider Vancouver context was that of environmentalism. Given Vancouver's international reputation for natural beauty, including the proximity to the Pacific Ocean and old-growth rainforest on the North Shore Mountains, those intending to lead Christian communities in the city must recognize the missional implications of sharing the gospel in a place where environmentalism is known as a "civil religion." Christian initiatives in this book espoused viewpoints and named practices that reflected a commitment to care for creation. It is important to note that there was no evidence that this commitment by Christians was somehow instrumentalized for the sake of mission or evangelism. In other words, it was not apparent that Christians were engaging in their commitment to creation care simply in order to proclaim the gospel. Instead, Christian initiatives in Vancouver articulated a sincere and deeply held theological value reflecting the biblical mandate for stewardship of creation that also offered overlapping consensus with their non-Christian neighbours holding values of "reverential naturalism." Residential, practice-based (e.g., advocacy, recreation, and farming) Christian communities in Vancouver, such as A Rocha or Christian outdoor camps, were often named by focus group participants as ideal examples of how Christians should be caring for the earth. Christian leaders in Vancouver would be wise to carefully attend to this shared value of environmentalism between their congregants and non-Christian neighbours as an opportunity to work together to build the common welfare of the city. Here too we see a link with the theological framework of exile as in Jeremiah 29:5, "Build houses and settle down; plant gardens and eat what they produce." For those in exile, they are to engage the natural surroundings in which God has placed them, including the tending and care of the earth. For Christians in a post-Christian context like Vancouver, a missional embrace of God, neighbour, and creation can properly be understood as a doxological act of Christian praise and practice. As Stefan Paas notes, "if mission is about God being glorified in all his creation, nothing can remain untouched,"[12] encouraging Christians to have a more wholistic understanding of mission where joining our neighbours in care for the planet is seen as an act of glorifying God as much as worship in a sanctuary.[13]

3 Mission through Walking Worthily

For those looking for insights from the research on how best to engage in Christian mission in Vancouver, an outcome suggested by this study is the need to attend to the wholistic impact of the Christian community through what the Bible calls "walking worthily."[14] Christians in this study clearly articulated their awareness of the negative aspects of the church's colonial mission activities, as well as the need to engage in a humble, peace-seeking way of witness in the world today that strives for reconciliation with all people. The growing awareness in the broader public (including through the media) of the church's participation in the government-mandated cultural genocide against Indigenous Peoples in the nineteenth and twentieth centuries through the Residential Schools program must be accounted for in order to engage in mission today. As a result, Christians in this Vancouver study could be described as, in Peter Schuurman's language, "reflexive." While Schuurman uses the phrase specifically in connection with evangelicals, I would argue that across denominational lines there is evidence in the data that Christians interviewed had a deep awareness of the problematic image of Christianity (spoiled identity) and therefore act in a "reflexive" manner whereby they are "not only highly self-conscious of their faith and its public perception, but are troubled by the stigmatization" that comes with Christianity identity as perceived by a wider, secular Canadian culture.[15] As messengers of the gospel of peace and reconciliation, Christians in Vancouver participating in this research acknowledged that God is calling them to walk worthily of the message they carry. Here, Christian pastors would be wise to model and equip their members for a wholistic approach to witness described by Seattle-based missional theologian Darrell Guder as "be, do and say" witness.[16] This invitation for Christians to approach "the other" with humility and grace through attention to their character (being), action (doing), and speech (saying) will be essential. The integrity of the gospel is questioned now in the broader Vancouver public due to the *previous* character, actions, and words of early Christians on the West Coast.

This new reality, where the church is declining in power while other people groups such as Indigenous or LGBTQI are increasing in prominence and influence, creates an urgency in the way in which Christians conduct themselves in the city. The biblical call to walk worthily is one that Christian communities in Vancouver must attend to in the way worship, small groups, service, and fellowship are utilized to help shape Christian character in the broader, more secular context of the city. Urban missiologists like David Fitch have been advocating this kind of wholistic formation for some time now.[17] While Christians may feel marginalized or forgotten in Vancouver, surrounded by a more secular (and at times perceived to be hostile) urban landscape, here too we see connections with the theme of exile. For the Jewish people in Babylon, they were also feeling isolated and surrounded by those who did not wish them well. However, Jeremiah's prophetic pronouncement of God's presence and purpose for them in exile gave the people hope for a sustained time of dislocation. Jeremiah 29:11 says, "'For I know the plans I have for you,' declares the Lord, 'plans to prosper you and not to harm you, plans to give you hope and a future.'" So too, Christian communities in Vancouver can find their way forward as a minority voice with affection for the surrounding community rather than retreating from public life in fear.

4 Mission through the Future Church that Is Coming

Finally, for those discerning through this research what God is up to in Vancouver and seeking guidance on how to respond in mission, it is important to note how the data identifies the way in which the face of Christianity is changing in the city. Canadian sociologists of religion have been noting this transition for some time now. Sam Reimer and Michael Wilkinson conclude from their extensive research with over five hundred pastors across Canada that "we see few reasons to think that any native-born Christian population will grow, including evangelicals. These numbers may stabilize depending on future immigration patterns and retention."[18] It appears when reflecting on the data that while many churches with European roots are aging and declining numerically in Vancouver, Christian churches with immigrant populations are growing in notable numbers and influence. Paul Bramadat and David Seljak have raised the point that "what is puzzling is the fact that (the) common and intimate relationship between Canadian Christianity and Canada's various ethnic communities has not yet received comprehensive treatment by scholars of Canadian religion or ethnicity."[19] Bramadat and Seljak note that "it often surprises people to learn how many of the 'visible minorities' they might see in their cities – including many of the Chinese, some of the South Asian, many of the Arab, most of the West Indian, and most of the African Canadians – are also Christians."[20] More research will be needed to help identify and analyze the characteristics and challenges of these non-European ethnic expressions of Christianity in Canada. Therefore, Christian leaders would be wise to mark that the future face of Christianity in Vancouver appears to be significantly different in ethnic composition than in the previous century. If this is the church that God is bringing to the West Coast, how might Christians respond? The research demonstrated that the impact of immigration, especially from Asia, is having a positive influence on most Christian initiatives in the fieldwork.[21] This was evident not only in the ethnic-specific churches studied or the pan-Asian multi-site evangelical congregations but also in the mainline Protestant and Catholic parishes profiled. How might leaders of Christian communities attend to this opportunity? While most Christian communities visited in the fieldwork described their fellowship as a "warm," "friendly," or "hospitable" space for others, this would need to be tested against a newcomer's actual experience. While most participants in this study espoused beliefs of welcome, inclusivity, and hospitality for all, there is much required for a cross-cultural experience of integrating and catechizing newcomers from different language and cultural backgrounds. Christian leaders would be wise to carefully study their initiative's practices and interview newcomers from different cultural backgrounds in order to create space that is truly inclusive and welcoming of others quite different than those already in the fellowship. This invitation to the newcomer and corresponding hospitality is a costly practice, for by doing so the original community itself will need to adapt how they relate to one another in worship (language, music, etc.) as well as fellowship and service.

Not all Christian communities will be able to make this change. Existing churches that continue to decline in numbers and vitality will have another way to make a significant, sacrificial contribution to the church that God is bringing – through creative use of real estate. The research also identified the pressing issue of scarce sacred space since Vancouver struggles with some of the most expensive real estate and living costs in the world. For congregations that currently own property but are experiencing decline, a challenge in the near future will be what to do with their building. Will their decision-making evidence "walking worthily" as they take their final footsteps as a community of faith? Many churches have already sold their lucrative real estate to developers to build condos where communion tables once stood. Some of these have negotiated smaller worship spaces (Oakridge United Church) while others have arranged for concessions of affordable housing in addition to for-profit housing (e.g., Central Presbyterian Church's redevelopment in downtown Vancouver[22]). For the church that God is bringing, however, affordable public assembly spaces for church plants is already a significant challenge. How might established congregations in Vancouver that are moving into a palliative stage of their journey be able to imagine the stewardship of their property beyond the current default practice of contracting with a developer to replace church buildings with high-rise condos? Could these declining congregations offer a final witness to the gospel that proclaims death and resurrection by gifting their multi-million-dollar property to other churches, mainly ethnic congregations and church plants growing and seeking space, in order to continue a witness not of their own but one carried out by future generations not yet born? Here again, we see connections with the theological framework of exile, where the people were encouraged to plan for a future they may not even live to see. Jeremiah 29:6 says, "Marry and have sons and daughters; find wives for your sons and give your daughters in marriage, so that they too may have sons and daughters. Increase in number there; do not decrease." The exiles were commanded by God to attend to the next generation (and generations after) by creating the conditions for life, even as they felt their own slipping away. For those leading Christian communities today in Vancouver, might they hear a similar summons from God to create space for Christian life to flourish for generations not yet born who might hear, receive, and respond to the gospel call of discipleship?

5 Contributions to the Missional Church Conversation

While set within an urban context of Canada's pre-eminent West Coast, this book's research also endeavoured to contribute to the ongoing discussion of mission within the wider North American context. What may be of lasting value to that broader missional theology conversation remains to be seen, of course, so at this time I humbly offer a few suggestions.

First, the call of the missional church to participate in the *missio Dei* will involve a more robust equipping of disciples for their witness in the world as we move deeper into post-Christendom. This research suggests that as Christians increasingly find themselves a minority within a larger, more secular urban context (with neighbours sometimes ambivalent and other times hostile towards the church), Christian initiatives will need to invest heavily in equipping their members for witness. If the Christendom church was at risk of outsourcing the baptismal vows of Christians to professional clergy, then a post-Christendom church must apprentice their baptized members to Jesus in such a way that Christians understand their own daily interactions with others in the neighbourhood as a key (and possibly only) connection between Christianity and their secular neighbour. Here I do not mean rolling out flashy evangelism programs or the latest bible study program from a Christian publisher in United States. Rather, the missional church must invest in deep and sustained catechesis in order to help call, form, and gird baptized believers as they practice their faith in a post-Christian landscape, offering God praise through their words and works. Christian identity formation within a wider world of powerful and competing allegiances will be an important practice for the missional church. This call for deeper catechesis finds resonance in recent scholarship, including Alan Kreider's *The Patient Ferment of the Early Church*.[23] Like the exiles in Babylon, core identity formation, rooted in listening and following God's commandments while remaining open to the wider world around them, will be an important part of faith formation moving forward. Stefan Paas notes that Jewish communities in diaspora attracted both converts (proselytes) and god-fearers (what he calls "guest members") more or less spontaneously without an active policy of recruitment.[24] Paas argues that the missionary vision of these Jewish diaspora communities included a combination of a liturgical, future-orientated, and centripetal vision.[25] With this in mind, missional churches will need to attend to this question of deep catechetical formation in an exile-like post-Christian West, rather than the previous Christian default of numeric growth, financial stability, and access to public power that I have named in a previous publication as "noses, nickels, and renown."[26] Instead, a ministry of hospitality and invitation to discipleship within Christian community has the potential to form believers who navigate their faith commitments in a post-Christendom landscape (walking worthily) while also serving as a witness to a waiting, watching world.[27]

Second, this study contributes to the wider missional conversation by highlighting the increasing need for Christians to confess and seek reconciliation in light of colonial mission actions that have caused real and ongoing harm to our neighbours. In particular, the emerging influence of the Indigenous Peoples of Canada upon public life, popular culture, and government policy means that Christians in the missional church movement in Canada need to attend to the systemic or corporate sin that Christians have participated in as part of their neighbourhood exegesis. Throughout this study, Christian initiatives (both leaders and members) articulated a sincere desire to build or repair relationships with local Indigenous Peoples, giving a new understanding to one's sense of place. Creating space for lament and the offering and receiving of forgiveness is important, along with a thoughtful and theological reading of both Scripture and context for decolonizing the church's witness. How are Christian initiatives in the wider missional church movement helping Christians understand, own, and work for reconciliation where past witness has brought harm? How might the missional church movement help clarify the essence of the good news to share with others, without continuing to make Western culture normative and a prerequisite for becoming a Christian today?

While the missional church movement has placed great significance on the local neighbourhood and its corresponding exegesis of place, this research encourages missional congregations to read text and context in the parish beyond the usual geographic, economic, or demographic lenses. Instead, the findings of this book encourage missional congregations to understand their parish with an awareness of settler culture and a decolonized reading of place in order to respectfully identify with, and be shaped by, the local Indigenous Peoples' understanding of land, sea, and sky. Indeed, missional congregations are called both to understand the church's complicit role in past racist policy (in Canada the primary focus may be on Indigenous Peoples; in the United States on the history of slavery with African Americans) and to be proactive in the joining of God's mission for shalom in the world, participating daily in a ministry of forgiveness and reconciliation with the eschatological vision of the healing of the nations. With growing attention now being paid to the colonial impact of mission, and its concurrent questions of race, gender, and privilege, the current missional church movement must also contend with the critique that its recognizable leadership (Roxburgh, Fitch, Frost,

Hirsch, Hastings, Van Gelder, Hagley, and Stetzer) is overwhelmingly male and Western (Caucasian). This call for the missional church movement to address issues of colonialism embedded in mission practice not only offers a needed prophetic role beyond the emphasis on the local but also holds the potential for welcoming a more diverse leadership in the movement.

Third, while the missional church conversation has focused on discerning God's agency in human culture and community, this study raises further questions regarding how Christians can discern and describe the *missio Dei* at work beyond an anthropocentric reading of culture to include creation. While Christian theology has a category for natural or general revelation, it is often depicted as the "opening act" for the emphasis upon special revelation in Israel and Christ. To date, there is a surprising lack of missional church literature on the question of *missio Dei* and general revelation in creation. Yet, the data in this research demonstrates that the Christian community's care for creation is a place of significant connection and engagement with their non-Christian neighbour. From trendy, leafy green neighbourhoods of Kitsilano to hardscrabble postal codes like the Downtown Eastside, participants in a variety of settings all placed a high value on creation as a place of beauty and God's revelation. While there is a long academic engagement in the study of eco theology (McFague, Hallman, Wilson, and Deane-Drummond), this study invites further integration of the missional church discussion with those who are wrestling with human stewardship of creation amidst the ongoing climate crisis. Furthermore, this desire to have the missional church movement attend to the urgent call for creation care brings with it a prophetic edge that at times appears to be muted, as noted above in reflection on colonial history. "Joining God in the neighbourhood" slogans of missional church gatherings will need to guard against a myopic view of proximity in order to place a focus on the local within the wider global challenge of a sustainable planet and humanity's impact on all forms of life.

CONCLUSION

As we reach the end of this book more questions remain regarding the nature of Christian witness in Canada's largest Pacific Rim city. Through a study conducted over several years, we have addressed the research question by offering observations in the last two chapters that include some normative outcomes for those seeking to provide an effective Christian witness in Vancouver. We identified the way in which Vancouver Christian initiatives were befriending a spiritual but not religious culture and placing a priority on developing deep relationships while building hospitable, alternative communities of Christian belonging in a city well known for its social isolation. Next, we identified the need for Christian initiatives to address the growing affordable housing crisis in the city as an act of missional engagement and connection with others. Furthermore, we reflected on the models of Christian witness, noting the emphasis Vancouver Christians place on the close-knit ties within community, which correspond closely with the Neighborhood Incarnation and New Community models identified by Christopher James's research in nearby Seattle.

Next, we marked how the research clearly identified Vancouver Christians' self-awareness of the impact of colonial history and the ongoing legacy of mistreatment of Indigenous Peoples in the name of the church. This awareness is shaping the way Christians worship and witness in the community, adopting a posture of humility, seeking forgiveness, and actively addressing reconciliation with Indigenous Peoples.

Then, we explored how the research data suggests that the face of Christianity is rapidly changing in the city, with a growing impact from ethnic churches, primarily from Asia. In addition, we identified a key finding from this research: the growing challenge for Christian witness due to a decreasing amount of already-scarce sacred space. As many Vancouver churches decline and close, fewer places are available for Christians to gather, including worship space for new expressions of Christian community such as immigrant churches or church plants. As well, the data showed a priority by Vancouver Christians to join with their non-Christian neighbours in reverence for and care of creation. Articulating a particular Christian theology of creation is understood to be both an alternative narrative to offer Vancouverites and a hopeful approach to the world during this time of climate crisis.

Turning from these observations to outcomes, we addressed the research question by exploring a theological framework of exile and suggested ways in which Christian leaders could build on this research for their practice in Vancouver. Mission through relationships as well as care for creation, equipping Christians to walk worthily, and attention to the changing face of Christianity were all explored as significant learnings from the research for the wider church and academia. Finally, these findings were put in conversation with the ongoing missional church movement in North America with suggestions on how the data from this study might further discussion on mission in the West.

Throughout the research for this book, participants, both church leaders and lay people, acknowledged the challenge of being a Christian as a minority within the larger population in this modern, secular West Coast city. Vancouver pastor Tim Dickau summarizes the challenge when he writes, "most church leaders I know feel as if the rug has been pulled out from under their ecclesiastical feet. Moreover, because belief has been optional and religion has been sidelined in the public sphere, the voice of the church has been effectively muted, making a life that is devoted to God seem irrelevant if not ludicrous." Dickau continues: "Like the dark, dense, suffocating cloud cover that often hangs over Vancouver's Pacific coastline in the winter, the secularity Charles Taylor describes can cast gloom and doubt over long-standing followers of Christ."[28] And yet, as this book draws to a close, I must also say how encouraged and impressed I was by the variety of thoughtful, innovative, and faithful people I met seeking the peace and prosperity of the city, while also continuing to offer a faithful witness, trusting that they were doing so in partnership with the triune God in their midst.

Earlier in this book, we attended to Noah Toly's question of how we reckon with the complexity of modern cities from a Christian perspective. By addressing the research question, we attempted a thicker description of Christianity in Vancouver today, and by doing so witnessed many Christians quietly at work trying to make a faithful impact on their neighbourhoods and city. In response to his own question, Toly says: "We ought to develop neighborhoods that signify and symbolize the reconciliation of God, humanity, and nature, and not only the estrangement between them. We must stretch and sacrifice and strive to live in ways that do not burden vulnerable ecosystems, far-off communities, and future generations."[29] In this book we have seen concrete examples of how Vancouver Christians are addressing this call to action that Toly demands. In building an urban missiology for Vancouver, we now have a clearer vision of the motivating beliefs and spiritualities of Christian communities, along with the cultural and organizational performances of missional engagement those communities exercise within the city of Vancouver.

The research for this book serves as an example of Christianity's minority report within a larger, more secular culture that bears little evidence of a Christendom legacy.

Therefore, while Vancouver, with its soaring mountains, old-growth forest, and ocean waves, remains a "super, natural" place for most residents, for those who claim their identity in baptismal waters with Jesus, the city remains both a place of God's revelation and a context for God's ongoing mission in a world in need, as ever, of reconciliation, hope, and peace.

Appendix

Fourteen Christian Communities
Participating in Vancouver Study

Artisan Church
Vancouver Japanese Language School and Japanese Hall,
487 Alexander Street, Vancouver, BC V6A 1C6
Non-denominational, former Mennonite Brethren
http://artisanchurch.ca

Cathedral of Our Lady of the Holy Rosary
646 Richards Street, Vancouver, BC V6B 3A3
Roman Catholic
www.holyrosarycathedral.org

First Christian Reformed Church
2670 Victoria Drive, Vancouver, BC V5N 4L2
Christian Reformed Church of North America
https://firstvan.ca

Jacob's Well
543 Powell Street, Vancouver, BC V6A 1G8
Non-denominational
www.jacobswell.ca

Kitsilano Christian Community
1708 West 16th Avenue, Vancouver, BC V6J 2M1
Canadian Baptists of Western Canada
www.kitschurch.com

Oakridge United Church
306 West 41st Avenue, Vancouver, BC V5Y 2S4
The United Church of Canada
https://oakridgeunited.org

Pacific Grace Mennonite Brethren Church
2855 East 1st Avenue, Vancouver, BC V5M 1A9
Mennonite Brethren
www.pgmbc.com

Sanctuary Mental Health Ministries
P.O. Box 20147 Fairview, Vancouver, BC V5Z 0C1
Non-denominational
www.sanctuarymentalhealth.org

St Gregory the Illuminator Armenian Orthodox Church
13780 Westminster Highway, Richmond, BC V6V 1A2
Armenian Orthodox Diocese of Canada
www.stgregorychurch.ca

St Paul's Anglican Church
1130 Jervis Street, Vancouver, BC V6E 2C7
The Anglican Church of Canada
www.stpaulsanglican.bc.ca

St Peter's Fireside
UBC Robson Square/Vancouver Art Gallery,
800 Robson Street, Vancouver, BC V6Z 3B7
Anglican Network in Canada
www.stpetersfireside.org

Tapestry Church–Marpole
Scottish Cultural Centre, 8886 Hudson Street,
Vancouver, BC V6P 4N2
Christian Reformed Church in North America
https://marpole.thetapestry.ca

Tenth Church–Kitsilano
1100 Chestnut Street, Vanier Park in Kitsilano,
Vancouver, BC V6J 3J9
Christian and Missionary Alliance
www.tenth.ca

Vancouver Chinese Presbyterian Church
6137 Cambie Street, Vancouver, BC V5Z 3B2
Presbyterian Church in Canada
www.vancpc.ca

Notes

1 Canadian author Allan Fotheringham is said to have given Vancouver this nickname, drawing from Greek mythology and pointing towards the city's hippie history, New Age reputation, and outdoor-focused lifestyle.
2 Luke 13:11.
3 A version of this story appears in the preface to Lockhart, ed., *Christian Witness in Cascadian Soil.*
4 Marketing Communications, Destination BC, www.destinationbc.ca/content/uploads/2018/08/Our-Brand.pdf
5 According to Government of Canada statistics, published from the 2021 National Household Survey conducted by Statistics Canada, Christianity has a minority status (29.89 per cent) in the city of Vancouver (population 662,248) compared to the larger category of residents describing themselves as having "no religion." For a reasonable scope and scale, this study focuses on the city of Vancouver, rather than the Greater Vancouver region that includes over 2.6 million inhabitants.
6 Cascadia refers to the Pacific Northwest geographic zone of North America that includes Oregon, Washington State, and British Columbia covered by the Cascade mountain range. The three largest Cascadian cities are Portland, Seattle, and Vancouver. Scholars suggest these two states and one province have shared values such as the environment, rugged individualism, high mobility, commitment to justice, broad spirituality without connection to particular religious traditions, and respect for Indigenous culture. For further reading, see Block, *The Secular Northwest.*
7 As James argues, "the church in a post-Christian context cannot rely on predominant culture to nurture people even halfway toward a way of life

constant with the Reign of God. The church in such an environment must be, and is, a conversion community." James, *Church Planting in Post-Christian Soil*, 222–3.

8 Reimer, *Evangelicals and the Continental Divide*, 132.

9 Ibid., 124.

10 Bramadat, Killen, and Wilkins-LaFlamme, eds, *Religion at the Edge*.

11 The language of "acting" here recognizes that within the Christian community itself the notion of agency is one that must consider a combination of both human and divine agency.

12 Pete Ward describes thick description in qualitative research as the kind of knowledge gained through study of particular communities that yields insight into the multi-layered and rich nature of social life. Ward, *Introducing Practical Theology*, 161.

13 While missiologists like Glenn Smith in Quebec City, John Bowen in Hamilton, and Christopher James in Seattle have focused on churches and church planting in urban contexts, there is little equivalent research here in Vancouver.

14 Sheldrake, *The Spiritual City*, 195. Sheldrake also reminds us that the word "secular" (Latin *saeculum*), unlike the word "profane," with which it is often confused, does not have any connotations of being radically opposed to the sacred. "In fact, the concept of the 'secular' has Christian origins and is simply the shared, common, public space of 'the present age' or the here and now" (27).

15 Biney, Ngwa, and Barreto, eds, *World Christianity, Urbanization, and Identity*, 4.

16 Thiessen, *The Meaning of Sunday*, 127.

17 Ibid., 129–46.

18 Bass, *The Practicing Congregation* (Herndon: Alban Institute, 2004), 12. This cultural displacement forced formerly mainline churches to focus inward, according to Butler Bass, dealing with issues of identity, vision, resources, and organization, often with great conflict and smothering self-doubt.

19 Butler Bass draws on the work of sociologist Paul Heelas and defines detraditionalization as a set of processes, variously described as "post-traditional" or "post-modern," whereby received traditions no longer provide meaning and authority in everyday life. Using Heelas language, she describes the shift of authority from "without" to "within," whereby voice is displaced from established sources, coming to rest in the self.

20 Marks, *Infidels and the Damn Churches*, 112.

21 Daly, *God Doesn't Live Here Anymore*, 137.

22 Seattle-based journalist and Christian minister Anthony Robinson has even joked that what appears to be snow on the top of the Rocky Mountains dividing Cascadia from the rest of North America is the "torn up baptismal certificates" of pioneers heading further west.

23 Marks, *Infidels and the Damn Churches*, 7.

24 Block, *The Secular Northwest*, 2. In her scholarly treatment of religion in Cascadia, Block argues that historically, "Northwesterners were part of a regional culture that placed relatively little importance on formal religious connections."

25 Ibid., 48.

26 The Angus Reid Institute, "A Spectrum of Spirituality: Canadians Keep the Faith to Varying Degrees, but Few Reject It Entirely," 13 April 2017, http://angusreid.org/religion-in-canada-150/#part-2.

27 In *A Secular Age* Canadian philosopher Charles Taylor works through the impact of secularity comparing western life in 1500 to 2000. Taylor explores secularity's impact in public spaces, decline in religious belief and practice, and the conditions of belief.

28 In *Faith in the Public Square* the former Archbishop of Canterbury makes the distinction between procedural and programmatic secularism. Procedural secularism, the kind that I refer to above, is secularism that gives equal voices to all manner of religious and political thought. Programmatic secularism attempts to eliminate religious voices from the public realm and for that Williams charges liberal modernity with being a fixed concept that approaches a new "pseudo-religion."

29 Paas, "Missional Christian Communities in Conditions of Marginality," 145.

30 Taylor, *A Secular Age*, 3.

31 Clarke and Macdonald, *Leaving Christianity*, 11.

32 Statistics Canada defines generations in the following way: Greatest Generation: people aged 94 or older (born before 1928); Interwar Generation: people aged 76 to 93 (born between 1928 and 1945); Baby Boomer Generation: people aged 56 to 75 (born between 1946 and 1965); Generation X: people aged 41 to 55 (born between 1966 and 1980); Generation Y (millennials): people aged 25 to 40 (born between 1981 and 1996); Generation Z: people aged 9 to 24 (born between 1997 and 2012);Generation Alpha: people aged 8 or younger (born between 2013 and 2021). https://www12.statcan.gc.ca/census-recensement/2021/as-sa/98-200-X/2021003/98-200-X2021003-eng.cfm.

33 Ibid., 171.

34 Ibid., 210.

35 Statistics Canada, Profile Table, www12.statcan.gc.ca/census-recensement/2021/dp-pd/prof/details/page.cfm?Lang=E&SearchText=Vancouver&DGUIDlist=2021A00055915022&GENDERlist=1&STATISTIClist=1&HEADERlist=0. Canada collects data on religion not according to "membership" but rather by the person's self-identification as having a connection or affiliation with any religious denomination, group, body, sect, cult, or other religiously defined community or system of belief. Religion is not limited to formal membership in a religious organization or group. Persons without a religious connection or affiliation can self-identify as atheist agnostic or humanist or can provide another applicable response.

36 Religion for the population in private households – 25 per cent sample data, according to Statistics Canada.

37 As Christopher James argues, "the church in a post-Christian context cannot rely on predominant culture to nurture people even halfway toward a way of life consonant with the Reign of God. The church in such an environment must be, and is, a conversion community." James, *Church Planting in Post-Christian Soil*, 222–3.

38 Personal correspondence, June 2019.

39 Personnel correspondence, May 2019.

40 Jonathan Wilson, "Beloved Community as Missional Witness," in Lockhart, ed., *Christian Witness in Cascadian Soil*, 177.

41 Lisa Slayton and Herb Kolbe, "Wholeness and Human Flourishing as Guideposts for Urban Ministry," in Drew, Boddie, and Peters, eds, *Urban Ministry Reconsidered*, 75.

42 Byassee and Lockhart, *Better than Brunch*, 100. See also Byassee, Chu, and Lockhart, *Christianity*.

43 Strhan, *Aliens and Strangers*, 35.

44 Bibby, Thiessen, and Bailey, *The Millennial Mosaic*, 251.

45 Bibby, *Resilient Gods*, 220–1.

46 John Longhurst, "'Dire' Report Projects Near End of Anglican Church in Canada," *The Winnipeg Free Press*, 12 November 2019, www.winnipegfreepress.com/arts-and-life/life/faith/dire-report-projects-near-end-of-anglican-church-in-canada-564814062.html.

47 Daly, *God Doesn't Live Here Anymore*, xvii.

48 Raymond J. de Souza, "Raymond J. de Souza: Covid May Have Hastened Christianity's Decline in Canada," *National Post*, 23 May 2021, https://nationalpost.com/opinion/raymond-j-de-souza-covid-may-have-hastened-christianitys-decline-in-canada.

49 Scharen, *Fieldwork in Theology*, 27.

50 I will use the language of Christian initiatives throughout this book to recognize that Christian communities include established congregations, church plants, and para-church Christian agencies.

51 Wellman and Corcoran, "The Precarious Nature of Cascadia's Protestants," in *Religion at the Edge*, 166.

52 Bibby, *Resilient Gods*, 221.

53 Soong-Chan Rah raises questions like this in his publications such as *Many Colors* and *The Next Evangelicalism*.

54 Adogame and Spickard, *Religion Crossing Boundaries*, 7–20. Adogame and Spickard identify patterns named Ellis Island (assimilation to the dominant culture), religious bi-localism (establishing institutions that keep connection with the home country while integrating with dominant culture), religious cacophony (resisting dominant culture and providing an alternative voice), reverse mission (cultures that once received missionaries from the West are now sending missionaries to the West), South-South religious trade (where religious communities in the global South send missionaries to another country in the global South – in Canada this can also mean non-Western missionaries to Indigenous communities), transnational organization theory (diverse ethnic and national voices bring unexpected agenda items from economic to power issues), and de-territorialized religious identity (a diaspora community that shares dislocation as a common element of uniting through religious practice).

55 Swinton and Mowat, *Practical Theology and Qualitative Research*, 25.

56 Ward, *Introducing Practical Theology*, 7. While Simon Chan and others would argue for "spiritual theology" as a middle step between systematic (precise terms to define the Christian faith) and practical theology (concerned with life in relation to the world), in which we focus on the life in relation to God, I am treating practical theology here in broader terms that incorporates the communities experience of the living God as integrated into its lived experience of the world around it.

57 Richard Osmer, "Empirical Practical Theology," in Cahalan and Mikoski, eds, *Opening the Field of Practical Theology*, 61.

58 Swinton and Mowat, *Practical Theology and Qualitative Research*, 257.

59 Ammerman, *Congregation & Community*, 47. By congregational culture Ammerman means physical artifacts, patterns of activity, and the language and story that embellish those objects and activities with meaning.

60 McAlpine, Thiessen, Walker, and Wong, *Signs of Life*, 3.

61 Ibid., 14. The researchers give an example of this with the United Church of Canada stressing diversity above many other categories.

62 Ibid., 217.

63 Everts, *The Hopeful Neighbourhood*, 17.
64 Glenn Smith, "Key Indicators of a Transformed City: The Church in Dialogue with its Context – Observations from Montreal," www.direction.ca/resources (last accessed 13 January 2024).
65 Glenn Smith, "My Neighborhood Is Gentrifying! Where on Earth Does Urban Ministry Need to Go?" in *Vespas, Cafes, Singlespeed Bikes, and Urban Hipsters*, 274.
66 Scharen, *Explorations in Ecclesiology and Ethnography*, 2.
67 Scharen & Vigen, *Ethnography as Christian Theology and Ethics*, 31.
68 Ibid., 44.
69 Lichterman, *Elusive Togetherness*, 2–3.
70 Ibid., 44.
71 Ibid., 260.
72 Wigg-Stevenson, *Ethnographic Theology*, 2.
73 Ibid., 10.
74 Ibid., 20.
75 Ibid., 50.
76 Ibid., 59.
77 Ibid., 168.
78 Ibid., 174.
79 James, *Church Planting in Post-Christian Soil*, 7.
80 Ibid., 8–10.
81 Ibid., 11.
82 Ibid., 13.
83 Ibid., 138. At the same time the ethnographic/urban approach has also had a significant impact on the development of missional theology in North America in a mutually transformative process.
84 Ibid., 143.
85 Ibid., 238.
86 Silverman, *Interpreting Qualitative Data*, 9–11.
87 The research is limited to Christian communities within the geographical boundaries of the city of Vancouver active in 2018–22 who reflect the World Council of Churches' definition of baptism as articulated in *Baptism, Eucharist, and Ministry*.
88 Van Gelder, *The Missional Church in Perspective*, 22–3.
89 Key concepts to explore include secularization, innovation, globalization, entrepreneurial Christianity, post-denominationalism, neo-liberalism, media, and consumerism.
90 Leong, *Street Signs*, 15.
91 An example of a house church network in the Vancouver area is known as "Simple Churches," www.simplechurches.ca/communities.

92 Moschella, *Ethnography as Pastoral Practice*, 98.

93 James, *Church Planting in Post-Christian Soil*, 247.

94 Throughout the research, participants often used different acronyms regarding human sexuality and gender expression and identity. For further explanation of these terms, please see 2SLGBTQIA+ explained: https://students.ubc.ca/ubclife/were-queer-were-here-queer-trans-visibility-ubc. As a result, there are a variety of acronyms throughout the manuscript, including LGBTQ, LGBTQ+, and 2SLGBTQIA+.

95 Regarding data management, throughout the qualitative research elements of this project there was a careful securing of the data generated, including removal of any identifying information regarding the focus groups from documents stored digitally, as well as having password-protected files of any digital data stored on the researcher's computer. Any information identifying individuals was stored in a separate password-protected file along with pseudonyms used on transcripts and fieldnotes of focus groups interviews. Support for securing the data in this research project was provided by the Information Technology contract employees of St Andrew's Hall at the University of British Columbia.

96 Josh Grant, "Census Data Shows B.C. Is the Most Secular Province in Canada," 30 October 2022, www.cbc.ca/news/canada/british-columbia/bc-most-secular-province-1.6633935. As mentioned earlier in the chapter, Statistics Canada's data from the 2021 National Household Survey identifies Christianity as a minority belief system within a larger, more secular population – No religion or secular perspective (55.80 per cent), Christian (29.89 per cent), Buddhist (4.04 per cent), Muslim (2.75 per cent), Sikh (2.54 per cent), Hindu (1.94 per cent), Jewish (1.94 per cent). Statistics Canada, Census Profile, 2021 Census of Population Profile table, www12.statcan.gc.ca/census-recensement/2021/dp-pd/prof/details/page.cfm?Lang=E&SearchText=Vancouver&DGUIDlist=2021A00055915022&GENDERlist=1&STATISTIClist=1&HEADERlist=0.

CHAPTER TWO

1 As noted in chapter 1, according to Statistics Canada, Christians in 2021 had a minority status in the city of Vancouver (29.89 per cent) compared to the larger category of residents described as "no religion or secular perspectives." (55.80 per cent), Statistics Canada, Census Profile, 2021 Census of Population Profile table, www12.statcan.gc.ca/census-recensement/2021/dp-pd/prof/details/page.cfm?Lang=E&SearchText=Vancouver&DGUIDlist=2021A00055915022&GENDERlist=1&STATISTIClist=1&HEADERlist=0. When referring to Vancouver as

Canada's third-largest city, I am moving beyond the narrow field of study for this project of the city of Vancouver, and referencing Metro Vancouver, which includes neighbouring communities and is more than 2.7 million residents, placing Vancouver behind the Greater Toronto Area and the region that includes the communities that make up Montreal.

2 David Ley, "Christian Faith and the Social Sciences in a Postmodern Age," in Packer and Wilkinson, eds, *Alive to God: Studies in Spirituality*, 281.

3 Madden, *Being Ethnographic*, 37.

4 Wolterstorff, *Art in Action*, 82.

5 Doxa is here referring to the work of sociologist Pierre Bourdieu who used the term to speak of what is taken for granted in a particular society where "the natural and social world appears as self-evident."

6 Wellman Jr and Corcoran, "The Precarious Nature of Cascadian Protestants," in Bramadat, Killen, and Wilkins-Laflamme, eds, *Religion at the Edge*, 166.

7 Beyer and Ramji, *Growing Up Canadian*, 303.

8 R. Drew Smith, "Introduction," in Drew, Boddie, and Peters, eds, *Urban Ministry Reconsidered: Contexts and Approaches*, 10. Smith asks: "Are urban churches equipped for community organizing, policy advocacy, and cultural translation?" He also inquires whether urban ministries are willing and able to grant their context a careful reading and adjust their ministries in relation to the potential and possibilities this reveals, or whether they project or impose their institution-bound subjectivities and norms upon the context.

9 Strhan, *Aliens and Strangers*, 88.

10 Luhrmann, *When God Talks Back*, 315.

11 Lynn Marks, Public Lecture, The University of Washington, 28 May 2019.

12 Reimer, *Caught in the Current*, 172.

13 Lockhart, *Beyond Snakes and Shamrocks*, 15. While this default faith expression regarding the environment has led me to quip upon occasion that "the hardest part about preaching heaven in Vancouver is most people think they are already there," it is worth further investigation in the fieldwork.

14 Aldred, "The Land, Treaty, and Spirituality," 3. Aldred gives an example of the specificity of the land in Indigenous culture when he translates John 3:16 in his own Cree language to read, "God so loved the land that he gave his son." Aldred notes that "the land takes in land, oceans, rivers and lakes, plants and all creatures. Not a generic land, but a specific place, *a Cree world, Askiwina.*"

15 Patrick Keifert, "The Return of the Congregation to Theological Conversation," in Keifert, ed., *Testing the Spirits*, 24.

16 Smith, *American Evangelicalism*, 97.

17 Berger, *The Sacred Canopy*.

18 Smith, *American Evangelicalism*, 106.

19 Reimer, *Caught in the Current*, 22–3.

20 Ibid., 24.

21 Bevans, Schroder, and Luzbetak, "Missiology after Bosch," 69.

22 Biney, Ngwa, and Barreto, *World Christianity, Urbanization and Identity*, 3.

23 Scott Hagley, "Free for Mission: Missional Church and Ethnographic Fieldwork," *Ecclesial Futures* 1, no. 1 (June 2020): 92.

24 Ibid., 105.

25 Ibid., 106.

26 Ibid.

27 Everts, *The Hopeful Neighborhood*, 24.

28 Ibid., 98.

29 Hagley, *Eat What Is Set before You*, 73.

30 Ibid., 141.

31 Ward, *Liquid Church*, 88.

32 Fiddes, "Ecclesiology and Ethnography: Two Disciplines, Two Worlds?" in Ward, ed., *Perspectives on Ecclesiology and Ethnography*, 33.

33 Harris, *The End of Absence*, 17.

34 Anthropologists define fieldwork as "the process of interacting and gathering information at the site or sites where a culture-sharing group is studied." Sangaramoorthy and Kroeger, *Rapid Ethnographic Assessments*, 65.

35 Hagley, *Eat What Is Set before You*.

36 Wigg-Stevenson, *Ethnographic Theology*.

37 Riphagen, "Church-in-the-Neighbourhood."

38 Quick or rapid ethnographic study is a recognized methodology providing an efficient collection and dissemination of information in fieldwork. This quick or rapid ethnographic approach has its roots in international health and development, arising in the 1970s from a need to respond quickly to problems in communities where little data were available, local research capacity was often limited, and where the success of interventions required direct engagement and collaboration with local communities. For more information, see Sangaramoorthy and Kroeger's *Rapid Ethnographic Assessments* where they argue that "it is possible to take short-term, rapid research that remains grounded in ethnographic principles" (2). This

research is "primarily a qualitative research method that focuses on the collection and analysis of locally relevant data" (3).

39 Nancy Eisland and Stephen Warner, "Ecology: Seeing the Congregation in Context," in Ammerman et al., *Studying Congregations*, 43–8.

40 Following Swinton and Mowat's lead, I am making a distinction between interviews and conversations. Swinton and Mowatt note that "interviews are not synonymous with conversations" and instead define interviews as "concentrated human encounters that take place between the researcher who is seeking knowledge and the research participant who is willing to share their experience and knowledge." (Swinton and Mowatt, *Practical Theology*, 60). By walking interviews, I am drawing on the methodological approach of Johannes Riphagen's PhD dissertation "Church-in-the-Neighbourhood: A Spatio-Theological Ethnography of Protestant Christian Place-Making in the Suburban Context of Lunetten," 42.

41 Given that the fieldwork was conducted during the "fourth wave" of the COVID-19 pandemic, many churches in Vancouver remained online for their worship services and did not hold in-person gatherings. For those churches or agencies who were accessed online, the conversation with the pastor in step 1 was conducted as a walking conversation in the neighbourhood where the Christian initiative was located, to better gain a sense of the context of the ministry's context.

42 Bryman, Bell, Reck, Fields, *Social Research Methods*, 207. A focus group is defined as a semi-structured interview in which several people are interviewed together in order to learn about people's experiences and perceptions, group dynamics, and processes through which social groups make meaning.

43 Ibid., 213. Bryman et al. note that "conducting qualitative interview through video-conferencing technologies is still relatively new, but the COVID-19 pandemic has made them increasingly a feature of everyday life."

44 Sangaramoorthy and Kroeger, *Rapid Ethnographic Assessments*, 47. The number of participants within a focus group should ideally be between five and ten people, although focus groups with as few as four sometimes suffice.

45 Cameron, Richter, Davies, and Ward, *Studying Local Churches*, 31.

46 Bryman, Teevan, and Bell, *Social Research Methods: Second Canadian Edition*, 130–1.

47 Bryman, Bell, Reck, and Fields, *Social Research Methods*, 207. Bryman et al. suggest that the number of focus groups required for a particular study varies, but it generally ranges from ten to fifteen. That guideline

was considered when selecting the number of Christian initiatives to be studied in the group interview phase of the project.

48 Swinton and Mowat, *Practical Theology and Qualitative Research*, 32–3.

49 Hans Schaeffer, "Concrete Church: Qualitative Research and Ecclesial Practices," in Ward and Tveitereid, eds, *Theology and Qualitative Research*, 153.

50 Watkins, *Disclosing Church*, 35.

51 Darrell Guder, "Practical Theology and Missional Theology: How are They Related?" in Dean, Drury, Bertrand, and Root, eds, *Consensus and Conflict*, 111–15. Guder argues further that "in response to the proclamation of (the gospel), the Spirit gathers witnesses and forms them into communities to serve God's mission. The gathered life of witnesses displays, demonstrates, enfleshes the good news by the ways the community communicates the gospel both as narrative as well as action. That communication takes place in and through all the Spirit-empowered forms of service that missionally defined practical theology enables the community to investigate, research, generate and employ." Or as David Bosch noted, "the church is both a theological and a sociological entity, an inseparable union of the divine and the dusty." Bosch, *Transforming Mission*, 389.

52 Here we are attending to what Gregg Okesson notes as the tension in research of congregations between what he calls theology "proper" or explicit (voiced by the clergy) versus theology "ordinary" or implicit (expressed or embodied by the congregation members). Okesson, *A Public Missiology*, 27, 151–3.

53 Cameron, Bhatti, Duce, Sweeney, and Watkins, *Talking about God in Practice*, 53–6. Cameron and colleagues define normative theology as a particular tradition's understanding of scriptures, creeds, official church teachings, and liturgies. Formal theology is the theology of academia and theologians, as well as dialogue with other disciplines. The espoused voice of theology is the theology embedded within a group's articulation of beliefs, while the operant theology is the theology embedded within the actual practice of a group.

54 Watkins, *Disclosing Church*, 41.

55 Sarah Dunlop, "Visual Ethnography," in Ward and Tveitereid, eds, *Theology and Qualitative Research*, 421. Dunlop writes: "I propose that enabling people to express their lived theology through images will go some way toward revealing operant theologies, because the visual communicates something of the embodied, intuited, experience nature of faith" (421).

56 Personal Correspondence with Stefan Paas, 15 October 2021. Paas
further suggested building on Ward's image that a congregation might be
compared to a theological library rather than a theological book. Thus,
ethnography (or any empirical method aimed at gaining an understanding
of congregations) is like carefully reading through a pile of theological
books, and trying to make sense of this, that is, trying to come to some
sort of synthetic understanding from the data that is embodied and
communal response to revelation.

57 Bryman, Teevan, and Bell, *Social Research Methods: Second Canadian
Edition*, 162. In developing the interview guide I followed the wisdom of
Bryman et al., including that the guide should create a certain amount
of order, so that questions flow reasonably well but still allow for
changing the order of the questions and the impromptu asking of different
questions; include questions or topics that address the research questions;
and use language that is comprehensible and familiar to those being
studied. Questions included in the guide but not mentioned above include
basic collection of information (name, membership status, etc.) as well
as consent to participate in the research.

58 Campbell-Reed and Scharen, "Ethnography on Holy Ground,"
232–59. Campbell and Scharen write: "We distinguish confidentiality –
not telling someone else's story – from secrecy, which would restrict
participants from telling anyone outside the group anything about what
happened at the interview day. The former builds trust. The latter would
actually erode it. However, we also remind them of their responsibility
in helping to keep identities anonymous."

59 Mannik and McGarry, *Practicing Ethnography*, 108–12. Open coding is
understood to be a detailed reading of the data, with minute attention to
detail on a word-by-word and line-by-line basis. Focused coding refers
to review and refining of open codes identified earlier, exploring the
interrelationships among the repeated codes. Selective coding involves
rereading the data in order to determine the key concepts and "theoretical
generation" that identifies key themes or issues that emerge from this
detailed study of the data. Bryman (et al.) refer to this three-fold process
as "open, axial and selective" coding.

60 Nancy Ammerman et al., *Studying Congregations*, 9.

61 Coffey, 1999; Holt, 2003.

62 Mannik and McGarry, *Practicing Ethnography*, 160. The authors note
how autoethnography has a growing place in the social sciences in
Canada with the 2012 conference of the Canadian Anthropology
Society (CASCA) focused on this theme. The autoethnographic aspects

of my research were primarily connected to being a professing Christian pastor and professor entering into Christian space and dialogue in Vancouver.

63 Bryman, Teevan, and Bell, *Social Research Methods: Second Canadian Edition*, 152.

64 Swinton and Mowat, *Practical Theology and Qualitative Research*, 24. As Swinton and Mowat observe, "practical theology is a fundamentally missiological discipline which receives its purpose, motivation and dynamic from acknowledging and working out what it means to participate faithfully in God's mission."

65 Bryman, Teevan, and Bell, *Social Research Methods: Second Canadian Edition*, 132–4.

66 Sheldrake, *The Spiritual City*, 117.

67 One pastor remarked that "if in the pre-pandemic era I considered a 'regular' attender to be once a month, who knows what that will mean after the pandemic? Will they even come back or have they already 'ghosted out' online?" As one might expect, humorous stories were exchanged between clergy about intentional or accidental faith conversations shared with their more agnostic neighbours in Vancouver. One pastor laughed as he recounted a recent exchange when someone asked him what he did for a living. "I said I was a pastor, and the guy had no idea what that even meant. I said to him, 'You know, like a minister,' to which the man said, 'Oh, you work for the government, like a cabinet minister.'" The other pastors laughed. "Not *that kind* of minister," joked another leader in the room. Another said in a more serious tone, "I rarely wear a clergy collar, but I do when I visit the hospital. In other places that I've served in Canada, the collar is usually met with approving nods. Here in Vancouver, clerical wear is met by people on the street with either confusion or even outright hostility."

CHAPTER THREE

1 Christopher James developed four models of Christian community based on his study of church plants in Seattle: Great Commission Team, Household of the Spirit, New Community, and Neighborhood Incarnation.

2 Bowen, *Green Shoots*, 193. Roxburgh writes that "this is not about the heroic leader with a planned future, but rather about detectives of divinity, attending to the clues of how the Spirit is forming the kingdom in the midst of the everyday."

3 Canadian Conference of Mennonite Brethren Churches, www.mennonite-brethren.ca/directory/c2c-network/ and C2C Collective, https://c2ccollective.com.

4 James, *Church Planting in Post-Christian Soil*, 172. "New Incarnation churches believe they have been sent with a comprehensive task on a limited scale (renewal of all things ... within the parish)." The vision of Artisan Church is explained on the website as meaning, "Vancouverites transformed into followers of Jesus, practicing His way and becoming like Him in every sphere of life. Our deepest desire is to be changed and to create change through Community Formation, Spiritual Formation, and Ministry Formation."

5 Artisan Church, https://artisanchurch.ca/about/vision/.

6 The Japanese Hall is a national historic site originally built in 1906 and renovated for community services in 2000. Artisan Church started in the Vancouver Library's downtown branch before moving to the Mount Pleasant neighbourhood and finally settling in the Downtown Eastside, a neighbourhood known for both its homeless population (and corresponding Christian missions) as well as a gentrifying dimension of high-rise condo dwellers.

7 The longest teaching time of any initiative visited in this study.

8 Hagley, *Eat What Is Set before You*, 254.

9 John Longhurst, "Successful Outreach Led to LGBTQ Inclusion," *Anabaptist World*, 9 April 2021, https://anabaptistworld.org/successful-outreach-led-to-lgbtq-inclusion/. The decision created significant attention and consternation within the Mennonite Brethren Conference. Artisan Church states on their website: "Gay? Straight? Same sex attracted (SSA)? Trans? Queer? Celibate? Unsure? Whatever language describes you best, you are welcome here. Artisan Church aims to hold non-judgmental space for the many perspectives on gender and sexuality, and we gladly welcome all LGBTQ+ and SSA siblings to fully participate with us in worship and ministry."

10 Artisan Church, http://artisanchurch.ca/about/lgbtq/.

11 James, *Church Planting in Post-Christian Soil*, 272.

12 John Longhurst, "Asked to Repent, LGBTQ-Welcoming Church Withdraws," *Anabaptist World*, 16 March 2021, https://anabaptistworld.org/asked-to-repent-lgbtq-welcoming-church-withdraws/.

13 Pastor Nelson described how he now finds himself in the position of fielding calls from other church leaders who want to lead their congregations in a pro-inclusion direction, but who are uncertain of how to do so without causing a rift within the membership or with a wider denominational body.

14 Artisan Church, https://artisanchurch.ca/about/partners/.
15 James, *Church Planting in Post-Christian Soil*, 166. Artisan Church's
   emphasis upon the "use and support of the creative arts" is another mark
   of the New Community in James's model.
16 St Peter's Fireside, www.stpetersfireside.org/story/. Their story is described
   in this way: We have a story. It's not tidy. It is more like working with
   charcoal. We are messy like our namesake. While Jesus was on trial,
   St Peter denied knowing him not once, but three times. He wept bitterly,
   alone in his failure, as Christ headed to the cross. Yet after the resurrection we discover the most beautiful scene. Peter isn't alone, he is with
   Jesus. They are sharing breakfast on the shores of Galilee. Jesus
   meets Peter with love, forgiveness, and most of all grace. As grace gets
   into Peter's bones and settles in his soul, his calling is renewed: Jesus
   sends him out into the world to share this good, beautiful, and entirely
   true story of resurrection, love, forgiveness, and most of all grace.
17 St Peter's Fireside, www.stpetersfireside.org/story/.
18 During the first year of the COVID-19 pandemic, the University's campus
   was closed and the church plant met in another part of Vancouver at
   a Seventh-day Adventist church before returning to their original site
   in September 2021.
19 Wilkins-Laflamme defines a religious Millennial as one with the highest
   probability of being religiously affiliated, and of believing in God
   according to the teachings of their religion.
20 Wilkins-Laflamme, *Religion, Spirituality and Secularity among*
   Millennials, 60. Wilkins-Laflamme has a fourth typology class – the
   non-religious Millennial that she defines as having very high probabilities
   of religious non-affiliation and the lowest of religious behaviour, as well
   as highest probabilities of uncertainty surrounding beliefs and indifference
   towards beliefs.
21 Unlike Artisan Church's pro-inclusion statement, St Peter's Fireside does not
   mention the church plant's position on human sexuality (including in the
   annual report published on the website), leaving one to either be informed
   already of this split in the Anglican Communion or do further investigation.
22 Killen and Silk, *Religion and Public Life in the Pacific Northwest*, 91.
   While Killen and Silk describe "sectarian entrepreneurs" as having "conservative Christianity with a 'happy face' that does not frequently advertise its
   theological exclusiveness" (p. 90), St Peter's Fireside is known for engaging
   directly on questions of mental health, including through the personal
   experience of depression shared openly by founding priest Alastair Sterne.
23 Paas, *Church Planting in the Secular West*, 54.

24 Wilkinson, "Evangelicals in the Pacific Northwest," in Bramadat, Killens and Wilkins-Laflamme, eds, *Religion at the Edge*, 200.

25 James, *Church Planting in Post-Christian Soil*, 156. James describes this modelling of an alternative community and desire to evangelistically reach out as duty: "the goal of the practice is satisfaction of the evangelist's personal obligation before God." Key practices of witness and mission at St Peter's Fireside were identified by focus group members as including a regular offering of the Alpha program, an annual "Carols in the City" public event in the downtown to share the gospel, and a monthly commitment by their small group ministries to partner with a local Christian mission or charity in service of neighbour.

26 Pitt, *Church Planters*, 21–2.

27 The congregation is identified as belonging to a denomination that united streams of the Methodist, Presbyterian, Congregational, and the Evangelical United Brethren Church in Canada. The congregation's "Mission and Vision" is described as Deep Spirituality, Bold Discipleship, Daring Justice.

28 Business in Vancouver, "Pandemic Accelerates $5B Oakridge Centre Overhaul," 24 August 2021, https://biv.com/article/2021/08/pandemic-accelerates-5b-oakridge-centre-overhaul.

29 Oakridge United Church was the product of multiple amalgamations over the years of various congregations in the area that closed and consolidated into the former building. In 2019, the congregation, in consultation with the United Church's Pacific Region judicatory, negotiated a development deal on the property. The older church building was torn down and a multi-storey condo tower was built on the sight. The congregation gave over ownership of the land to the new condominium strata corporation and retains the air parcel rights for the first floor of the new development, with fourteen underground parking spaces designated for church use.

30 However, the congregation that was in decline for many years, has continued to get smaller during the COVID-19 pandemic. Rev. Joy James told me the congregation today has "about fifteen regular worshippers and about forty-five listed on the membership roll."

31 Sheldrake, *The Spiritual City*, 129. Sheldrake argues that "religious buildings are, if you like, 'texts' in the sense that we can read their sign systems and interpret their meaning."

32 James, *Church Planting in Post-Christian Soil*, 170.

33 With such a small number of people in the congregation I expected to hear more urgency in adding to their numbers, but with strong financial

support from the sale of the property it may remove some concern about how to maintain the ministry.

34 Matthew Hedstrom, "The Transformation of Religion," in Heft and Stets, eds, *Empty Churches*, 195.

35 Wellman Jr and Katie Corcoran, "The Precarious Nature of Cascadia's Protestants," in Bramadat, Killen, and Wilkins-Laflamme, eds, *Religion at the Edge*, 181.

36 St Paul's Anglican Church, www.stpaulsanglican.bc.ca/about. The church's website espouses: "As a part of the Anglican Church of Canada, the worldwide Anglican Communion and in the universal Church, we proclaim and celebrate the transforming gospel of Jesus Christ in worship and action!"

37 St Paul's Anglican Church, www.stpaulsanglican.bc.ca/about/history. In 1998 the parish formally sought permission from the diocesan bishop to perform (same-sex) blessings. St Paul's began the campaign for inclusion by seeking support from other parishes at the annual diocesan synod. This was obtained when a slim majority voted in favour of the initiative. In the circumstances the bishop moved with care, but as support grew from year to year the bishop granted the requested permission in 2002. This led to significant consequences not only for St Paul's and the Anglican Church of Canada but also for the whole global Anglican Communion.

38 Ammerman, *Congregation & Community*, 171.

39 James, *Church Planting in Post-Christian Soil*, 289.

40 The congregation originally met in a dance hall saloon near Broadway and Kingsway before moving to its current location on the northwest corner of 10th Avenue (thus its name Tenth) and Ontario Street.

41 The website describes the growth of Tenth since Pastor Ken Shigematsu's arrival this way: Since 1996, Tenth Church has grown from a community of 175 people to more than 2,000, making it one of the largest and most diverse city-centre churches in Canada. Our community includes immigrants, students, and young families; artists, entrepreneurs, and professionals; the urban poor and people on the margins of society. The staff listing is the largest of any church studied in this book with forty-four people, Ken Shigematsu being listed first as senior pastor. Of these staff, only two are designated for the site of this study – Tenth Kits – Dan Matheson as site pastor and Danielle Blond as pastoral support. The overall team of forty-four are roughly 50 per cent Caucasian and 50 per cent persons of colour, with most of those being Asian-Canadian.

42 Tenth Church, www.tenth.ca/pages/about.

43 James, *Church Planting in Post-Christian Soil*, 171.

44 Pastor Matheson described the approach as something like a traffic light – red light, yellow light, green light. When he gathers regularly with the other site pastors and the senior leadership, there are certain "red light" non-negotiables of doctrine and the "brand" of Tenth Church that they have in common. Then there are "yellow light" areas where people can ask for guidance on ministry projects or partnerships, receiving feedback from the other pastors. Pastor Matheson noted this was extremely helpful to him, having a group of trusted colleagues who helped make his ideas better. Finally, there are "green light" issues of worship leadership, small group ministry, and so forth where the campus pastors are free to direct as they choose.

45 Tenth Church describes its impact on the broader city in the following way: "We are known for our ability to communicate the gospel in a way that engages people at various places on their spiritual journey, including those on the borderlands of faith. Tenth Church has been recognized in various media for our commitment to justice, demonstrated in ministries such as outreach to the homeless and advocacy on behalf of women and children vulnerable to the sex trade both in Vancouver and internationally."

46 Tapestry–Marpole describes itself as "a multi-ethnic, multi-generational church centred in Christ and living for the glory of God. We are a community woven in faith, inspired by hope and motivated by love."

47 Pastor Jesse Pals described the logistics of setting up and taking down sound equipment, children's program material, and hospitality items each week as demanding. They purchased a twenty-one-foot trailer to hold all the equipment that was stored at the Tapestry–Richmond site and would arrive early each Sunday morning at the movie theatre.

48 Pastor Jesse Pals did not use "crowd" in a pejorative way, saying that Jesus spoke to "crowds" all the time in the gospels, but only some were committed followers. The core of about one hundred and fifty people, including many families, had easily made the switch to the new location. Pastor Pals celebrated that Tapestry–Marpole was turning five years old and commented on how grateful he was to be part of the larger multi-site staff team of the Tapestry Church that offered mentoring and support.

49 James, *Church Planting in Post-Christian Soil*, 173.

50 The website clearly identifies the congregation in many places as belonging to the Mennonite Brethren Canadian Conference and the BC Conference of Mennonite Brethren Churches.

51 James, *Church Planting in Post-Christian Soil*, 88.

52 Hardy and Longo, "Developmental Perspectives on Youth Non-affiliation," in Heft and Stets, eds, *Empty Churches*, 142.

53 First Christian Reformed Church, https://firstvan.ca/about/ The aims of the church are further developed on the website under four categories: Sustained in Worship (worship draws us in as diverse peoples and unifies our purpose under Jesus), Formed in Christ (discipleship development), Made for Relationship (focused on relationship with God and neighbour, including refugees in the community), and Here for Good (rooted in the neighbourhood to make a difference).

54 First Christian Reformed Church, https://firstvan.ca/about/.

55 Immigrant Services Society of British Columbia, https://issbc.org.

56 James, *Church Planting in Post-Christian Soil*, 179. "Key NI [New Incarnation] practices of hospitality, disciplined attention to place, and focused listening to the people around them seem destined to become increasingly important aspects of the witness the church can offer as an 'alternative society.'"

57 Deanna Ferree Womack, "Converting Mission: Interfaith Engagement as Christian Witness," in Flett and Congdon, eds, *Converting Witness*, 183.

58 The sanctuary of Fairview Baptist Church seats four hundred people; however, the congregation that owns the building and gathers later on Sunday mornings for worship is smaller than Kitsilano Christian Community. Before the pandemic, Kitsilano Christian Community worshipped with between eighty to one hundred people. Today, there are about thirty people who gather in person, with another twenty-five worship participants online.

59 Since Kitsilano Christian Community and Fairview Baptist Church congregations belong to the same denomination, there were many who thought the two might amalgamate over the years. However, Pastor McKinlay suggested that the relationship of "landlord/tenant" has remained unchanged.

60 James, *Church Planting in Post-Christian Soil*, 169.

61 Barrett, *Treasure in Clay Jars*, xiii.

62 James, *Church Planting in Post-Christian Soil*, 37.

63 Carol Ann MacGregor and Ashlyn Haycook, "Lapsed Catholics and Other Religious Non-Affiliates," in Heft and Stets, eds, *Empty Churches*, 85.

64 Like Holy Rosary Cathedral, St Gregory's was difficult to connect with Christopher James's four models from Seattle. The ethnic-specific and cultural focus of St Gregory's sets it apart from the models developed by James.

65 Links are provided to further explore the history of the Armenian church and a whole section is dedicated to telling the story of the 1915 Armenian genocide and the Vancouver memorial dedicated in 2016. Information is also provided on the denominational links working down from the Catholicosate to the Prelacy in Canada to the local parish.

66 "Commemoration of 103rd Anniversary of Armenian Genocide Mountain View Vancouver, BC," *Horizon*, 23 April 2018, https://horizonweekly.ca/ en/commemoration-of-103rd-anniversary-of-armenian-genocide-mountain-view-vancouver-bc/.

67 Cameron, *Talking about God in Practice*, 148.

68 This is an example of a prayer from Session One: I am not here to pass judgment or point the finger at anyone. My name was written in the sand as one who is forgiven. Strengthened with hope, impervious to shame, I will walk freely like the freshness of the dry lands after rain. Let light spill out of heaven through my life, dispelling mediocrity and silent blame. Too many people, guilt-stricken, wounded, walk in regret, feeling bad about failing, apologise even for breathing. Raw belief, a passion for others grows in me, encircling each moment with instinctive prayer. I will carry the freshness of the dry lands after rain. Compassion lives in me again. Amen.

69 Black, Indigenous and People of Colour.

70 Cameron, *Talking about God in Practice*, 130.

71 "Vancouver's Oppenheimer Park Empty of People and Tents, Officials Clean Site," Canadian Broadcasting Corporation, 10 May 2020, www. cbc.ca/news/canada/british-columbia/vancouver-s-oppenheimer-park-empty-of-people-and-tents-officials-clean-site-1.5563919.

72 Jacob's Well, www.jacobswell.ca. The five-minute video locates the ministry in the Downtown Eastside of Vancouver on the unceded territories of the xwməθkwəy̓əm (Musqueam), Sḵwx̱wú7mesh (Squamish), and Səl̓ílwitulh (Tsleil-Waututh) nations and offers a glimpse into the life of Jacob's Well with interviews of various community members and images of their activities together.

73 Jacob's Well describes its theological convictions in this way on the website: "Our theological differences do not drive us apart but challenge us to love each other in the midst of tension, and to be respectful, gracious and generous in conversation. We believe our common purpose as followers of Christ is to announce the good news (Gospel) of the Kingdom of God, a Kingdom of justice and shalom, where nothing is missing or broken, where all things are reconciled and restored. We do this in word and action, longing and working for right relationships between God, ourselves, our fellow humans, and creation."

74 Strhan, *Aliens and Strangers*, 108.
75 James, *Church Planting in Post-Christian Soil*, 172.
76 Strhan, *Aliens and Strangers*, 106.
77 Mechteld Jansen, "Christian Mission and Secularism," in Kim,
    Jorgensen, and Fitchett-Climenhaga, eds, *The Oxford Handbook of
    Mission Studies*, 494.
78 McAlpine, Thiessen, Walker, and Wong, *Signs of Life*, 224.
79 James, *Church Planting in Post-Christian Soil*, 136.
80 Ibid., 104.
81 Wilkinson, "Evangelicals in the Pacific Northwest," in Bramadat,
    Killens and Wilkins-Laflamme, eds, *Religion at the Edge*, 192.
82 Strhan, *Aliens and Strangers*, 89.
83 Black, Indigenous and People of Colour.

CHAPTER FOUR

1 Toly, *Cities of Tomorrow and the City to Come*, 22.
2 Sheldrake, *The Spiritual City*, 196.
3 Henry and Henry, *Be Kind, Be Calm, Be Safe*.
4 Graham, *Apologetics without Apology*, 3.
5 Wellman Jr and Corcoran, "The Precarious Nature of Cascadia's
   Protestants," in Bramadat, Killens and Wilkins-Laflamme, eds, *Religion
   at the Edge*, 168.
6 Thiessen and Wilkins-LaFlamme, *None of the Above*, 86. In developing
   this category of spiritual but not religious, they write: "Regardless of
   whether people self-identify, solicited or unsolicited, as spiritual but not
   religious, there is a substantial portion of nones who have beliefs and
   behaviour that we would classify as SBNR. For the 'spiritual' component
   of the label, we focus here on individual self-identification as very or
   moderately spiritual, since the term can include a whole variety of beliefs
   and practices. For the 'but not religious' component, we exclude
   individuals who frequent religious services regularly."
7 Sarah Wilkins-Laflamme, "Second to None: Religious Non-affiliation
   in the Pacific Northwest," in Bramadat, Killen, and Wilkins-Laflamme,
   eds, *Religion at the Edge*, 109.
8 This finding in the Vancouver research echoes the findings of Hans
   Riphagen in the Netherlands and Paul Lichtermann in the United States
   of America.
9 Authors attributed to the New Atheist perspective include Sam Harris,
   Richard Dawkins, Daniel Dennett, and Christopher Hitchens.

10 Thiessen and Wilkins-LaFlamme, *None of the Above*, 77.

11 Nancy Ammerman, "The Many Meanings of Non-Affiliation," in Heft
    and Stets, eds, *Empty Churches*, 49. Ammerman explores the diversity
    of those who are non-religious, including through social class. She writes:
    "a significant number of unaffiliated people are neither the well-educated,
    well-off Sunday brunch crowd nor former members of religious communi-
    ties where disaffiliation can neatly be defined in terms of organizational
    disconnection or loss of belief. Understanding the nones means first
    understanding that they are not all alike" (49).

12 Bramadat, "Reverential Naturalism in Cascadia," in Bramadat, Killens
    and Wilkins-Laflamme, eds, *Religion on the Edge*, 36.

13 The phrase "Vancouver chill" is the equivalent of the "Seattle freeze"
    identified in Christopher James's work, meaning a social phenomenon
    where urban residents are cold or unfriendly with a fake-polite exterior.

14 Reimer, *Caught in the Current*, 103. Reimer's research suggests that
    evangelicals still believe evangelism is an important Christian practice
    but tend to engage in it more as a group activity from the church, rather
    than as a personal practice.

15 McAlpine, Thiessen, Walker, and Wong, *Signs of Life*, 206.

16 James, *Church Planting in Post-Christian Soil*, 90. "Pastors noted the
    'Seattle Freeze' and widespread loneliness and see their missional commu-
    nities as presenting to these neighborhoods a faithful offer of belonging."

17 Riphagen, "Church-in-the-Neighbourhood," 299.

18 Ibid., 204.

19 James, *Church Planting in Post-Christian Soil*, 172. "NI [New
    Incarnation] participants relate to neighbors, first, as neighbors. That is,
    as fellow members of the community of foremost importance, their
    primary reference group is the neighborhood."

20 White and Wiley, *New Worshipping Communities*, 26.

21 This observation from the Vancouver research resonates with the work
    of missiologists such as Steven Bevans who describe a more prophetic
    approach to urban engagement in *Models of Contextual Theology* as the
    "countercultural model. Bevans, *Models of Contextual Theology*, 118.

22 Paas, "The Counter-Cultural Church," 295. Paas describes the main
    characteristics of the counter-cultural church as (1) Christianity is not a
    universalizing narrative that can be rendered intelligible and relevant for
    all of society, but rather a particular story rooted in a concrete history
    of God's people and accessible only through conversion and initiation;
    (2) the Christian message is not vindicated by its results in society or by
    its correspondence to generally accepted standards of rationality but

by the life of the Christian community; (3) the church's crucial mission is to form a holy people, a congregation that truthfully represents what the gospel is about in the face of an unbelieving world. (p. 284)

23 Ibid., 296.

24 Pouteaux, *The Bees of Rainbow Falls*, 27.

25 Guder, "The Theological 'Why' of Church Planting," in Lockhart, ed., *Christian Witness in Cascadian Soil*, 46.

26 As Rick Osmer notes, "a missional community is called together by God, built up, and sent into the world to bear witness to the gospel. This is its mission. Its purpose is not to serve as the chaplain of the culture, help parents raise moral children, keep young people out of trouble, meet the spiritual needs of adults, support civil society, and so forth. These are all important, but they are secondary goals or by-products of the church's primary mission: to bear witness to the gospel of Jesus Christ." Osmer, *The Invitation: A Theology of Evangelism*, 196.

27 Stone, *Finding Faith Today*, 48–9.

28 Root, *Churches and the Crisis of Decline*, 273.

29 McAlpine, Thiessen, Walker, and Wong, *Signs of Life*, 13.

30 Runyon and Pathak, *The Art of Neighboring*.

31 Pouteaux, *The Neighbours Are Real and Other Beautiful Things*, 63–4.

32 The Tyee, https://thetyee.ca/News/2020/08/19/Isolated-Neighbourhood-Couple-Planted-Seed/.

33 Riphagen, "Church-in-the-Neighbourhood," 204.

34 Ibid., 210.

35 Shigematsu, *Survival Guide for the Soul*, 168–9.

36 Riphagen, "Church-in-the-Neighbourhood," 213.

37 Beach, *The Church in Exile*, 198–9.

38 Reimer and Wilkinson, *A Culture of Faith*, 113.

39 Smith, *Wisdom from Babylon*, 16.

40 Demographia International Housing Affordability, http://demographia.com/dhi.pdf. Findings from the 15th Annual Demographia International Housing Affordability Survey 2019 surveying Australia, Canada, China (Hong Kong), Ireland, New Zealand, Singapore, United Kingdom, and United States. Authors of the report: Wendell Cox and Hugh Pavletich.

41 Real Estate Board of Greater Vancouver, www.rebgv.org.

42 Cassidy Oliver, "Student Owns $31.1-million Point Grey Mansion," *Vancouver Sun*, 11 May, 2016, http://vancouversun.com/storyline/student-owns-31-1-million-point-grey-mansion.

43 Bal Brach, "Vancouver Housing Prices Tweet Spurs 'DontHave1Million' Social Media Campaign," Canadian Broadcasting Corporation,

16 April 2015, www.cbc.ca/news/canada/british-columbia/vancouver-housing-prices-tweet-spurs-donthave1million-social-media-campaign-1.3036655.

44 Donaldson, *Land of Destiny*, 172.

45 Copeland, *City of Glass*, 156.

46 White, *Recovering: From Brokenness and Addiction to Blessedness and Community*, 15.

47 Marcus Gee, "What I Saw in a Day on the Downtown Eastside Shocked Me," *Globe and Mail*, 9 November 2018, www.theglobeandmail.com/canada/article-what-i-saw-in-a-day-on-the-downtown-eastside-shocked-me/.

48 Personnel correspondence, April 2019.

49 Community Builders, www.communitybuilders.ca.

50 James Heft, "Understanding and Responding to Non-affiliation," in Heft and Stets, eds, *Empty Churches*, 337.

51 Paul Bramadat, "Reverential Naturalism in Cascadia," in Bramadat, Killen, and Wilkins-Laflamme, eds, *Religion at the Edge*, 32.

52 Daly, *God Doesn't Live Here Anymore*, 174.

53 Douglas Todd, "Why Is British Columbia so Secular?" *Vancouver Sun*, 30 August 2017, https://vancouversun.com/news/staff-blogs/why-is-british-columbia-so-secular.

54 Vancouver Foundation, www.vancouverfoundation.ca/sites/default/files/documents/VanFdn-SurveyResults-Report.pdf.

55 One-third of the people surveyed said it is difficult to make new friends in Vancouver. One in four said they were alone more often than they would like to be. In both cases, people who experienced this also reported poorer health, lower trust, and a hardening of attitudes towards other community members.

56 While most Vancouverites surveyed reported the names of at least two of their neighbours, the connections typically stop there. Most did not do simple favours for neighbours (like taking care of their mail when they are away) and fewer had visited a neighbour's home or invited a neighbour over. One-third of the people surveyed did not know if their neighbours trusted each other. And barely a majority thought that the ties in their neighbourhood were growing stronger.

57 The research suggested it was not a lack of time that stopped people from getting involved in community. Rather, the most often-cited reason for not participating in neighbourhood and community life was a feeling of having little to offer.

58 Over one-third of those surveyed had no close friends outside of their own ethnic group. The majority reported that people preferred to be with

others of the same ethnicity. Many respondents believed all new immigrants and refugees, regardless of where they came from, would be welcome in their neighbourhood. However, some residents ranked which groups they believed would be the most and the least welcome.

59 Most people reported that they believed Vancouver was becoming a resort town for the wealthy. These same people also tended to think that there was too much foreign ownership of real estate.

60 Vancouver Foundation, www.vancouverfoundation.ca/connectandengage/community-connections.

61 Tamara Baluja, Jennifer Wilson, "You Are Not Alone: Vancouverites Share Their Stories of Isolation." CBC News, 20 November 2018, www.cbc.ca/news/canada/british-columbia/you-re-not-alone-vancouverites-share-their-stories-of-loneliness-1.4913190.

62 Ashifa Kassam, "Is Vancouver Lonelier Than Most Cities or Just Better about Addressing It?" *The Guardian*, 4 April 2017, www.theguardian.com/world/2017/apr/04/vancouver-loneliness-engaged-city-taskforce-canada.

63 Dickau, *Forming Christian Communities*, 131.

64 Jonathan Bird speaking as part of a panel discussion at the Centre for Missional Leadership's "Affordable Housing Conference" at St Andrew's Hall, 2 April 2022.

65 Daly, *God Doesn't Live Here Anymore*, 153.

66 James, *Church Planting in Post-Christian Soil*, 172.

67 Benac, *Adaptive Church*, 5.

68 Ibid., 165.

69 Ibid., 124.

70 Pitt, *Church Planters*, 27.

71 Kyo Seong Ahn, "Christian Mission and Colonialism," in Kim, Jorgensen, and Fitchett-Climenhaga, eds, *The Oxford Handbook of Mission Studies*, 330–1.

72 Daly, *God Doesn't Live Here Anymore*, 98.

73 The Indian Act, https://indigenousfoundations.arts.ubc.ca/the_indian_act/ (last accessed 14 January 2024).

74 Gina Colvin and Rosemary Dewerse, "Christian Mission and Indigenous Peoples," in Kim, Jorgensen, and Fitchett-Climenhaga, eds, *The Oxford Handbook of Mission Studies*, 437.

75 Denominations that partnered with the Canadian federal government to operate residential schools include the Roman Catholic Church (44), the Anglican Church of Canada (21), the United Church of Canada (13), and the Presbyterian Church in Canada (2).

76 Joanne Pepper, "Do Missionaries Destroy Culture?" in Santos and Naylor, eds, *Mission and Evangelism in a Secularizing World*, 119.

77 Reimer, *Evangelicals and the Continental Divide*, 120.

78 Ibid., 21.

79 Wilkins-Laflamme, *Religion, Spirituality and Secularity among Millennials*, 163.

80 Daly, *God Doesn't Live Here Anymore*, 96.

81 Willow Fiddler and Tavia Grant, "What Indigenous Youth Heading to the Vatican for a Historic Visit with the Pope Want to Know," *Globe and Mail*, 26 March 2022, www.theglobeandmail.com/canada/article-what-indigenous-youth-want-the-pope-to-know/.

82 Eric Reguly and Tavia Grant, "Pope Francis to Tour Canada in July, with Stops in Edmonton, Quebec and Iqaluit," *Globe and Mail*, 13 May 2022, www.theglobeandmail.com/world/article-pope-francis-to-visit-canada-in-july-vatican-says/.

83 Schuurman, *The Subversive Evangelical*, 48.

84 Ibid., 48.

85 Glen Schaefer, "West End Sex Workers Honoured with Memorial," *Vancouver Sun*, 17 September 2016, https://vancouversun.com/news/local-news/west-end-sex-workers-honoured-with-memorial.

86 Sam Chaise, "Doing Things We Have Never Done Before," in Santos and Naylor, eds, *Mission and Evangelism in a Secularizing World*, 4.

87 Bosch, *Transforming Mission*, 227.

88 Sheldrake, *The Spiritual City*, 159.

89 Wesley Granberg-Michaelson, *Future Faith*, 63.

90 Mark MacDonald, "Indigenous and Anglican: A Truly Native Church Emerges in the Anglican Church of Canada," in Bolger, ed., *The Gospel after Christendom*, 317.

91 Lenard Monkman, "Historical Ban on Potlatch Ceremony Has Lingering Effects for Indigenous Women, Author Says," CBC News, 25 March 2017, www.cbc.ca/news/indigenous/historical-ban-spirituality-felt-indigenous-women-today-1.4036528 and Roshini Nair, "Totem Pole Raising 50 Years Ago Sparked 'Reawakening,' Haida Artist Says," CBC News, 25 August 2019, www.cbc.ca/news/canada/british-columbia/haida-totem-pole-anniversary-1.5256754. See also Indigenous politician and lawyer Jody Wilson-Raybould's reflections on potlatch and the matrilineal political and legal order of West Coast First Nations in Wilson-Raybould, *From Where I Stand*, 182.

92 Woodley, *Indigenous Theology and the Western Worldview*, 63 and 98. Woodley names the unique Indigenous contribution to Christian theology

as an interpretation of shalom he calls "the Harmony Way." He
describes the Harmony Way as consisting of: (1) Tangible spirituality/our
spirituality must be practiced (Respect everyone. Everything is sacred);
(2) Our lives are governed by harmony (Seek harmony); (3) Community
is essential (Increase your friends and family); (4) Humor is sacred and
necessary (Laugh at yourself); (5) Feeling of cooperation/communality
(Everyone gets a say); (6) Oral communications and traditions (Speak
from your heart); (7) Present and past time orientation (Look forward
by looking back); (8) Open work ethic (Work hard but rest well);
(9) Great hospitality/generosity (Share what you have); (10) Natural
connectedness to all creation (We are all related). Woodley, *Indigenous
Theology*, 92–4.

93 Oliver, *Holy Ignorance*, 120.
94 Personal correspondence, 13 January 2022.
95 McLeod and Ustorf, *The Decline of Christendom in Western Europe*, 11.
96 Claire Dwyer, "Transnational Religion, Multiculturalism and Global
Suburbs: A Case Study from Vancouver," in Garbin and Strhan, eds,
Religion in the Global City, 187.
97 Byassee, Chu, and Lockhart, *Christianity: An Asian Religion in
Vancouver*, 57.
98 Angus Reid Institute, https://angusreid.org/our-team/.
99 Personal correspondence, 8 February 2021.
100 Reimer, *Caught in the Current*, 168.
101 Thiessen, *The Meaning of Sunday*, 169.
102 Glen Schaefer, "Richmond Churches Push Back at Racist Flyers by
Organizing Rally," *Vancouver Sun*, 5 December 2016, https://vancouver-
sun.com/news/local-news/richmond-churches-push-back-at-racist-flyers-
by-organizing-rally.
103 Byassee and Lockhart, *Better than Brunch*, 28.
104 Andrew Faiz, "Why Over a Third of Canadians Now Claim to Have
No Religion," *Broadview*, 2 May 2023, https://broadview.org/
secularism-canada/.
105 Bakke, *A Theology as Big as the City*, 13.
106 Bibby, *Resilient Gods*, 217. While the limited scope of this project is
focused on Christian initiatives in the city of Vancouver, there is much
to learn in future study of the broader, multi-faith question within the
region connected to immigration. For example, in the nearby growing
suburb of Surrey (predicted to be larger in population than the city of
Vancouver by 2030), there is the largest Sikh population in North
America (180,000).

107 Rev. Joy James also noted the need for a clear sense of mission before redeveloped and that "the result too often is that you have the same, declining congregation simply transplanted into a new space."

108 Richard Pitt, *Church Planters*, 2.

109 Alyssa Hirose, "Vancouver Is Officially the Third Most Expensive City in the World to Build a House In (Great)," *BC Business*, 18 January 2022, www.bcbusiness.ca/Vancouver-is-officially-the-third-most-expensive-city-in-the-world-to-build-a-house-in-great.

110 Daly, *God Doesn't Live Here Anymore*, 164.

111 Makins, *Why Would Anyone Go to Church?* 16.

112 Sheldrake, *The Spiritual City*, 203.

113 Norman Wirzba questions the assumption named by some in our study, such as Oakridge United Church, regarding the value of a visible Christian presence when he writes that "the flip side of this scenario is that the continued visible presence of church buildings does not guarantee the presence of God. Nor does it assure us that the people inside them will live in a God-glorifying manner." Wirzba, *From Nature to Creation*, 9.

114 Garbin and Strhan, *Religion and the Global City*, 19.

115 United Church Real Estate division, https://united-church.ca/leadership/church-administration/united-property-resource-corporation, and Trinity Centres Foundation: https://trinitycentres.org.

116 Thiessen, *The Meaning of Sunday*, 159.

117 As noted by Bibby, *The Boomer Factor*, 2006.

118 Thiessen, *The Meaning of Sunday*, 158.

119 Bibby, *Mosaic Madness*, 9.

120 Sheldrake, *The Spiritual City*, 139–40. Sheldrake notes that what constitutes soul will be particular to each place. "Sometimes it will be a particular building, whether religious or not, sometimes it will be a historical monument or other symbol of a city's memories. However, it will often be a natural feature – for example a large central park or a river that runs through the city." For Vancouver, one could name everything from Stanley Park to the North Shore Mountains to the Fraser River or the Pacific Ocean at English Bay as significant places that represent the soul of the city.

121 Cheryl Chan, "Extinction Rebellion Plans Two-Week 'October Rebellion' in Vancouver Streets," *Vancouver Sun*, 9 October 2021, https://vancouver-sun.com/news/local-news/extinction-rebellion-plans-two-week-october-rebellion-in-vancouver-streets.

122 St Paul's Anglican Church, https://www.stpaulsanglican.bc.ca/about/our-beliefs.

123 Sheldrake, *The Spiritual City*, 182.

124 James, *Church Planting in Post-Christian Soil*, 172.
125 Wilson, *God's Good World*, 37.
126 Lockhart, *Lessons from Laodicea*, 49.
127 Wilson, *God's Good World*, 38.
128 The limited scope of this research did not enable me to engage in a more fulsome theological discussion on whether there is evidence of Vancouverites exhibiting either pantheism or panentheism viewpoints regarding nature, but it is worth further exploration.
129 Shibley, "Secular but Spiritual in the Pacific Northwest," in Killen and Silk, eds, *Religion and Public Life in the Pacific Northwest*, 157.
130 Bramadat, "Reverential Naturalism in Cascadia," in Bramadat, Killen, and Wilkins-Laflamme, eds, *Religion at the Edge*, 24.
131 Paas, *Pilgrims and Priests*, 200.
132 Williams, *Exiles on Mission*, 176.

CHAPTER FIVE

1 Silverman, *Interpreting Qualitative Data*, 9–11.
2 Swinton and Mowat, *Practical Theology and Qualitative Research*, 123.
3 Drawing on the disruptive relocation of God's people from Jerusalem to Babylon in the sixth century BCE, the theme of exile has been used often by Christians to describe the shift from the church connected to worldly power in Christendom to its new location on the margins in post-Christendom. In addition to mainline Protestant and missional church circles, the language of exile has also been used in conservative evangelical settings in the United States, often in a tone bordering on resentment. See Paas, *Pilgrims and Priests*, 130.
4 Brueggemann's works on the theme of exile include *Hopeful Imagination: Prophetic Voices in Exile* (1986), *Cadences of Home: Preaching among Exiles* (1997), and *Out of Babylon* (2010).
5 Paas, "Missional Christian Communities in Conditions of Marginality," 154.
6 Roxburgh, *Practices for the Refounding of God's People*, 121.
7 Paas, *Pilgrims and Priests*, 149.
8 Alpha Canada and the Flourishing Congregational Institute, *The Priority and Practice of Evangelism*, www.flourishingcongregations.org/_files/ugd/68e091_25df2ee227b64fcda1509ee01b0b757c.pdf.
9 Ibid.
10 Reimer, *Evangelicals and the Continental Divide*, 132. Reimer also notes significant differences in his research between American and Canadian evangelicals sharing a similar sub-culture, with Canadians evangelicals

not only demonstrating irenic characteristics but also demonstrating less emphasis on nationalistic identity as a significantly reduced connection between faith and politics.

11 Ibid., 133.

12 Paas, "Missional Christian Communities in Conditions of Marginality," 149.

13 Paas further explores the essential aspect of doxology for Christian mission in *Pilgrims and Priests*, 222–9. "Christians do good, not to be effective or create opportunities for success, but in order to glorify the generous, merciful God who has brought about the world out of nothing and who creates life out of death. They do not work on the basis of optimism, but on the basis of faith, hope and love" (227).

14 Colossians 1:10, Colossians 4:1, Ephesians 4:1, Philippians 1:27, 1 Thessalonians 4:1.

15 Schuurman, *The Subversive Evangelical*, 6.

16 Guder, *Be My Witnesses*, 146; Guder, *Called to Witness*, 132.

17 Fitch most fully develops his teaching on this in *Faithful Presence*, 40–3. Following Acts 4:26–27, Fitch argues that Christians live as a people in three circles: a close circle of worship in Christ's risen presence ("the Temple"), most often on Sunday; a dotted circle of presence in our neighbourhoods ("house to house"); and a half circle of presence among people who are not Christians ("favour with all people").

18 Reimer and Wilkinson, *A Culture of Faith*, 203.

19 Bramadat and Seljak, *Christianity and Ethnicity in Canada*, 4.

20 Ibid.

21 For further reflections, see the data from *Christianity: An Asian Religion in Vancouver*, a separate research project I engaged in with two colleagues interviewing Asian Christian lay people about their experiences of life, vocation, and faith in Vancouver.

22 Architizer, https://architizer.com/blog/projects/central-presbyterian-church-2/.

23 Kreider, *The Patient Ferment of the Early Church*, 156–61. Kreider notes specific practices in the early church's catechetical work that would be of benefit today, including "transforming the habitus," "avoiding idolatry," "learning the master narrative," "learning the teachings of Jesus," "memorizing biblical passages," "imitating role models," and "fostering a culture of peace."

24 Paas, *Pilgrims and Priests*, 145. Paas describes how god-fearers sympathized with the Jewish religion, keeping Sabbath and some food laws but were not circumcised. This category of god-fearer might

correspond to what many churches call "adherent" in Canada, where one is welcome to belong without making a formal commitment to the community of faith.

25 Ibid., 148. Paas explains: "Liturgical, because its emphasis was on worshipping God on behalf of all nations. Future-oriented, because they looked at the present (including the conversion of non-Jews) from the viewpoint of God's kingdom and the restoration of Israel. And centripetal, because they concentrated more on welcoming newcomers than on actively finding 'unreached' people."

26 Byassee and Lockhart, *Better than Brunch*, 76.

27 Canadian author and journalist Malcolm Gladwell offered an example of this by describing the counter-cultural witness of attending a friend's wedding at a small Mennonite church in Ontario that turned a typical receiving line into a service line. https://malcolmgladwell.bulletin.com/what-i-found-at-a-mennonite-wedding/ (last accessed 10 July 2022).

28 Dickau, *Forming Christian Communities in a Secular Age*, xxi.

29 Toly, *Cities of Tomorrow and the City to Come*, 22.

Bibliography

Abbot, Walter. *The Documents of Vatican II*. New York: Herder and Herder, 1966.

Adams, Michael. *Sex in the Snow: The Surprising Revolution in Canadian Social Values*. Toronto: Penguin, 2006.

Adogame, Afe, and James V. Spickard, eds. *Religion Crossing Boundaries: Transnational Religious and Social Dynamics in Africa and the New African Diaspora*. Boston: Brill, 2010.

Airhart, Phyllis. *The Church with the Soul of the Nation: Making and Remaking the United Church of Canada*. Montreal & Kingston: McGill-Queen's University Press, 2014.

– *Serving the Present Age: Revivalism, Progressivism, and the Methodist Tradition in Canada*. Montreal & Kingston: McGill-Queen's University Press, 1992.

Aldred, Ray. "The Land, Treaty, and Spirituality: Communal Identity Inclusive of Land." *Journal of NAIITS: An Indigenous Learning Community* 17, no. 1 (2019).

Allen, Richard. *The Social Passion: Religion and Social Reform in Canada, 1914–28*. Toronto: University of Toronto Press, 1973.

Ammerman, Nancy. *Congregation & Community*. Rutgers: Rutgers University Press, 1997.

Ammerman, Nancy, William McKinney, Carl Dudley, and Jackson Carroll. *Studying Congregations: A New Handbook*. Nashville: Abingdon, 1998.

Anderson, Donald, and Andrew Donaldson, eds. *The Book of Praise: Presbyterian Church in Canada*. Toronto: Oxford University Press, 1997.

Anderson, Kay. *Vancouver's Chinatown: Racial Discourse in Canada, 1875–1980*. Montreal & Kingston: McGill-Queen's University Press, 1991.

Atkin, John. *The Changing City: Architecture and History in Central Vancouver*. Vancouver: Stellar, 2010.

Bakke, Ray. *A Theology as Big as the City*. Downers Grove: IVP, 1997.

Barrett, Lois, ed. *Treasure in Clay Jars: Patterns in Missional Faithfulness*. Grand Rapids: Eerdmans, 2004.

Bass, Diana Butler. *The Practicing Congregation*. Herndon: The Alban Institute, 2004.

Beach, Lee. *The Church in Exile: Living in Hope after Christendom*. Downers Grove: IVP, 2015.

Bellah, Robert. *The Sacred Canopy: Elements of a Sociological Theory of Religion*. New York: Doubleday, 1967.

Benac, Dustin. *Adaptive Church: Collaboration and Community in a Changing World*. Waco: Baylor University Press, 2022.

Benesh, Sean, ed. *Vespas, Cafes, Singlespeed Bikes, and Urban Hipsters: Gentrification, Urban Mission, and Church Planting*. Portland: Urban Loft, 2014.

Bevans, Steven. *Models of Contextual Theology*, revised edition. Maryknoll: Orbis, 2004.

Bevans, Stephen, Roger Schroder, and LJ. Luzbetak. "Missiology after Bosch: Reverencing a Classic by Moving Beyond." *International Bulletin of Missionary Research* 29, no. 2 (2005).

Beyer, Peter, and Rubina Ramji. *Growing Up Canadian: Muslims, Hindus, Buddhists*. Montreal & Kingston: McGill-Queen's University Press, 2013.

Bibby, Reginald. *The Boomer Factor: What Canada's Most Famous Generation Is Leaving Behind*. Toronto: Bastian Books, 2006.

– *Mosaic Madness: Pluralism without a Cause*. Toronto: Stoddart, 1990.

– *Resilient Gods: Being Pro-Religious, Low-Religious or No Religious in Canada*. Vancouver: University of British Columbia Press, 2019.

Bibby, Reginald, Joel Thiessen, and Monetta Bailey. *The Millennial Mosaic: How Pluralism and Choice Are Shaping Canadian Youth and the Future of Canada*. Toronto: Dundurn, 2019.

Bilgrami, Akeel, ed. *Beyond the Secular West*. New York: Columbia University Press, 2016.

Biney, Mosey O., Kenneth N. Ngwa, and Raimundo C. Barreto, eds. *World Christianity, Urbanization, and Identity*. Minneapolis: Fortress Press, 2021.

Block, Tina. *The Secular Northwest: Religion and Irreligion in Everyday Postwar Life*. Vancouver: UBC Press, 2017.

Bolger, Ryan, ed. *The Gospel after Christendom*. Grand Rapids: Baker, 2012.

Bolsinger, Tod. *Canoeing the Mountains: Christian Leadership in Uncharted Territory*. Downers Grove: IVP, 2018.

Bosch, David. *Transforming Mission: Paradigm Shifts in Theology of Mission*, 20th anniversary edition. Maryknoll: Orbis Books, 2011.

Bowen, Glenn. "Grounded Theory and Sensitizing Concepts." *International Journal of Qualitative Method* 5, no. 3 (September 2006): 12–23.

Bowen, John, ed. *Green Shoots in Dry Ground: Growing a New Future for the Church in Canada*. Eugene: Wipf & Stock, 2013.

Bramadat, Paul, Patricia O'Connell Killen, and Sarah Wilkins-LaFlamme, eds. *Religion at the Edge: Nature, Spirituality and Secularity in the Pacific Northwest*. Vancouver: UBC Press, 2022.

Bramadat, Paul, and David Seljak, eds. *Christianity and Ethnicity in Canada*. Toronto: University of Toronto Press, 2008.

Bryman, Alan, Edward Bell, Jennifer Reck, and Jessica Fields. *Social Research Methods*. Oxford: Oxford University Press, 2021.

Bryman, Alan, James Teevan, and Edward Bell. *Social Research Methods: Second Canadian Edition*. Don Mills: Oxford, 2009.

Bush, Peter. *Western Challenge: The Presbyterian Church in Canada's Mission on the Prairies and the North, 1885–1925*. Winnipeg: Watson & Dwyer, 2000.

Butcher, Dennis, ed. *Prairie Spirit: Perspectives on The United Church of Canada in the West*. Winnipeg: University of Manitoba Press, 1985.

Byassee, Jason, Albert Chu, and Ross Lockhart. *Christianity: An Asian Religion in Vancouver*. Eugene: Cascade, 2023.

Byassee, Jason, and Ross Lockhart. *Better than Brunch: Missional Churches in Cascadia*. Eugene: Cascade, 2020.

Cahalan, Kathleen, and Gordon Mikoski, eds. *Opening the Field of Practical Theology: An Introduction*. New York: Rowman & Littlefield, 2014.

Calvin, John. *Institutes of the Christian Religion*. Louisville: Westminster/John Knox, 1960.

Cameron, Helen, Deborah Bhatti, Catherine Duce, James Sweeney, and Clare Watkins. *Talking about God in Practice: Theological Action Research and Practical Theology*. London: SCM, 2010.

Cameron, Helen, Philip Richter, Douglas Davies, and Frances Ward, eds. *Studying Local Churches: A Handbook*. London: SCM, 2005.

Cameron, Kim S., and Robert E. Quinn. *Diagnosing and Changing Organizational Culture: Based on the Competing Values Framework*, revised edition. San Francisco: Jossey-Bass, 2006.

Campbell-Reed, Eileen, and Christian Scharen. "Ethnography on Holy Ground: How Qualitative Interviewing is Practical Theological Work." *International Journal of Practical Theology* 17, no. 2, (2013).

Chalmers, Randolph. *See the Christ Stand: A Study in the Doctrine of The United Church of Canada.* Toronto: Ryerson, 1945.

Clarke, Brian, and Stuart Macdonald. *Leaving Christianity: Changing Allegiances in Canada since 1945.* Montreal & Kingston: McGill-Queen's University Press, 2017.

Clifford, N. Keith. *Resistance to Church Union in Canada: 1094–1939.* Vancouver: University of British Columbia Press, 1985.

Coupland, Douglas. *City of Glass: Douglas Coupland's Vancouver.* Vancouver: Douglas and McIntyre, 2000.

Daly, Michael Wood. *God Doesn't Live Here Anymore: Decline and Resilience in the Canadian Church.* Eugene: Cascade, 2023.

Davis, Chuck. *The History of Metropolitan Vancouver.* Vancouver: Harbour, 2011.

Dean, Kendra Creasy, Amanda Drury, Blair Bertrand, and Andy Root, eds. *Consensus and Conflict: Practical Theology for Congregations in the Work of Richard R. Osmer.* Eugene: Pickwick, 2019.

Dickau, Tim. *Forming Christian Communities in a Secular Age: Recovering Humility and Hope.* Toronto: Tyndale Academic, 2021.

Donaldson, Jesse. *Land of Destiny: A History of Vancouver Real Estate.* Vancouver: Anvil Press, 2019.

Everts, Don. *The Hopeful Neighbourhood: What Happens When Christians Pursue the Common Good.* Downers Grove: IVP, 2020

Fitch, David. *Faithful Presence: Seven Disciplines that Shape the Church for Mission.* Downers Grove: IVP, 2016.

Flett, John, and David Congdon, eds. *Converting Witness: The Future of Christian Mission in the New Millennium.* Lanham: Lexington/Fortress, 2019.

Foreign Missions of the Assemblies of God. "Brussels Statement on Evangelization and Social Concern." *Transformation* 16:2 (1999).

Foss, Michael. *Power Surge: Six Marks of Discipleship for a Changing Church.* Minneapolis: Fortress, 2000.

Francis I. Vatican. *Evangelii Gaudium: Apostolic Exhortation on the Proclamation of the Gospel in Today's World.* 24 November 2013.

Garbin, David, and Anna Strhan, eds. *Religion in the Global City.*
London: Bloomsbury Academic, 2017.

Goheen, Michael. *Introducing Christian Mission Today: Scripture,
History and Issues.* Downers Grove: IVP, 2014.

Graham, Elaine. *Apologetics without Apology: Speaking of God
in a World Troubled by Religion.* Eugene: Cascade, 2017.

Grandberg-Michaelson, Wesley. *Future Faith: Ten Challenges Reshaping
Christianity in the 21st Century.* Minneapolis: Fortress, 2018.

Grant, John Webster. *Volume Three of a History of the Christian Church
in Canada: The Church in the Canadian Era.* Toronto: McGraw-Hill
Ryerson, 1972.

Gregg, William. *History of the Presbyterian Church in the Dominion
of Canada.* Toronto: Presbyterian Publishing, 1885.

Guder, Darrell. *Be My Witnesses.* Grand Rapids: Eerdmans, 1985.

– *Called to Witness: Doing Missional Theology.* Grand Rapids:
Eerdmans, 2014.

– *The Continuing Conversion of the Church.* Grand Rapids:
Eerdmans, 2000.

– "Evangelism and Justice: From False Dichotomies to Gospel
Faithfulness." *Church & Society* 92, no. 2 (November–December 2001).

– "From Mission and Theology to Missional Theology." *The Princeton
Seminary Bulletin,* vol. XXIV, no. 1 (2003).

– *The Incarnation and the Church's Witness.* Eugene: Wipf & Stock, 1999.

– *Unlikely Ambassadors: Clay Jar Christians in God's Service.* Louisville:
Presbyterian Publication Service, 2002.

Hagley, Scott. *Eat What Is Set before You: A Missiology of the
Congregation in Context.* Portland: Urban Loft, 2019.

Hardy, Nancy, and Leonard Lythgoe, eds. *Voices United: The Hymn and
Worship Book of The United Church of Canada.* Etobicoke: The United
Church Publishing House, 1996.

Harris, Michael. *The End of Absence: Reclaiming What We've Lost
in a World of Constant Connection.* Toronto: Harper Collins, 2014.

Hastings, Ross. *Missional God, Missional Church: Hope for
Re-Evangelizing the West.* Downers Grove: IVP, 2012.

Hauerwas, Stanley. *In Good Company: The Church as Polis.* Notre
Dame: University of Notre Dame Press, 1995.

Hay, Eldon. *The Covenanters in Canada: Reformed Presbyterianism
from 1820 to 2012.* Montreal & Kingston: McGill-Queen's University
Press, 2012.

Heft, James, and Jan Stets, eds. *Empty Churches: Non-Affiliation in America*. Oxford: Oxford University Press, 2021.

Henry, Bonnie, and Lynn Henry. *Be Kind, Be Calm, Be Safe: Four Weeks that Shaped a Pandemic*. Toronto: Random House, 2021.

Hjalmarson, Leonard, ed. *The Soul of the City: Mapping the Spiritual Geography of Eleven Canadian Cities*. Portland: Urban Loft, 2018.

Hoekendijk, J.C. *The Inside Out Church*. Philadelphia: The Westminster Press, 1964.

James, Christopher B. *Church Planting in Post-Christian Soil*. Oxford: Oxford University Press, 2017.

Keifert, Patrick, ed. *Testing the Spirits: How Theology Informs the Study of Congregations*. Grand Rapids: Eerdmans, 2009.

Killen, Patricia O'Connell, and Mark Silk, eds. *Religion and Public Life in the Pacific Northwest: The None Zone*. Walnut Creek: Altamira, 2004.

Kim, Kirsteen, Knud Jorgensen, and Alison Fitchett-Climenhaga, eds. *The Oxford Handbook of Mission Studies*. Oxford: Oxford University Press, 2022.

King, Mike. *Postsecularism: The Hidden Challenge to Extremism*. Cambridge: James Clarke & Co., 2009.

Klempa, William. *Burning Bush and a Few Acres of Snow: The Presbyterian Contribution to Canadian Life and Culture*. Ottawa: Carleton University Press, 1994.

Kreider, Alan. *The Patient Ferment of the Early Church: The Improbable Rise of Christianity in the Roman Empire*. Grand Rapids: Baker, 2016.

Leong, David. *Street Signs: Toward a Missional Theology of Urban Cultural Engagement*. Eugene: Pickwick, 2012.

Ley, David. *Millionaire Migrants: Trans-Pacific Life Lines*. Oxford: Wiley-Blackwell, 2010.

Lichterman, Paul. *Elusive Togetherness: Church Groups Trying to Bridge America's Divisions*. Princeton: Princeton University Press, 2005.

Lockhart, Ross. *Beyond Snakes and Shamrocks: St Patrick's Missional Leadership Lessons for Today*. Eugene: Cascade, 2018.

– *Lessons from Laodicea: Missional Leadership in a Culture of Affluence*. Eugene: Cascade, 2016.

Lockhart, Ross, ed. *Christian Witness in Cascadian Soil*. Eugene: Cascade, 2021.

Long, Thomas G. *Testimony: Talking Ourselves into Being Christian*. San Francisco: Jossey-Bass, 2004.

Luhrmann, T.M. *When God Talks Back: Understanding the American Evangelical Relationship with God*. New York: Vintage, 2012.

Lyon, David, and Marguerite Van Die, eds. *Rethinking Church, State and Modernity: Canada between Europe and America*. Toronto: University of Toronto Press, 2000.

Madden, Raymond. *Being Ethnographic: A Guide to the Theory and Practice of Ethnography*. London: Sage, 2010.

Makins, Kevin. *Why Would Anyone Go to Church?* Grand Rapids: Baker, 2020.

Mannik, Lynda, and Karen McGarry, eds. *Practicing Ethnography*. Toronto: University of Toronto Press, 2017.

Marks, Lynn. *Infidels and the Damn Churches: Religion and Irreligion in Settler British Columbia*. Vancouver: UBC Press, 2017.

Marti, Gerardo, and Gladys Ganiel. *The Deconstructed Church: Understanding Emerging Christianity*. Oxford: Oxford University Press, 2014.

McAlpine, Bill, Joel Thiessen, Keith Walker, and Arch Chee Keen Wong. *Signs of Life: Catholic, Mainline and Conservative Protestant Congregations in Canada*. Toronto: Tyndale Academic Press, 2021.

McGavran, Donald. *Understanding Church Growth*. Grand Rapids: Eerdmans, 1990.

McLeod, Hugh, and Werner Ustorf. *The Decline of Christendom in Western Europe, 1750–2000*. Cambridge: Cambridge University Press, 2003.

Moir, John. *Christianity in Canada: Historical Essays*. Toronto: Redeemer Press, 2001.

– *Enduring Witness: A History of The Presbyterian Church in Canada*. Burlington: Eagle Press, 1987.

– *Volume Two: A History of the Christian Church in Canada: The Church in the British Era*. Toronto: McGraw-Hill Ryerson Press, 1972.

Moschella, Mary Clark. *Ethnography as Pastoral Practice: An Introduction*, 2nd edition. Cleveland: The Pilgrim Press, 2023.

Moyse, Ashley John. *The Art of Living for a Technological Age: Toward a Humanizing Performance*. Minneapolis: Fortress Press, 2021.

Newbigin, Lesslie. *The Gospel in a Pluralist Society*. Grand Rapids: Eerdmans, 1989.

– *The Open Secret: An Introduction to the Theology of Mission*. Grand Rapids: Eerdmans, 1995.

– *Unfinished Agenda: An Updated Autobiography*. Eugene: Wipf & Stock, 1993.

Nikolajsen, Jeppe Bach. *The Distinctive Identity of the Church: A Constructive Study of the Post-Christendom Theologies of Lesslie Newbigin and John Howard Yoder*. Eugene: Pickwick, 2015.

Okeja, Uchenna, ed. *Religion in the Era of Post-secularism*. London: Routledge, 2020.

Okesson, Gregg. *A Public Missiology: How Local Churches Witness to a Complex World*. Grand Rapids: Baker, 2020.

Oliver, Roy. *Holy Ignorance: When Religion and Culture Part Ways*. Oxford: Oxford University Press, 2013.

Osmer, Richard. *The Invitation: A Theology of Evangelism*. Grand Rapids: Eerdmans, 2020.

Paas, Stefan. *Church Planting in the Secular West: Learning from the European Experience*. Grand Rapids: Eerdmans, 2016.

– "The Counter-Cultural Church: An Analysis of the Neo-Anabaptist Contribution to Missional Ecclesiology in the Post-Christendom West." *Ecclesiology* 15, no. 3 (2019): 283–301.

– "Missional Christian Communities in Conditions of Marginality: On Finding a 'Missional Existence' in the Post-Christian West." *Mission Studies* 38 (2021): 143–62.

– *Pilgrims and Priests: Christian Mission in a Post-Christian Society*. London: SCM, 2019.

Packer, J.I., and Loren Wilkinson, eds. *Alive to God: Studies in Spirituality*. Grand Rapids: Eerdmans, 1992.

Pitt, Richard. *Church Planters: Inside the World of Religion Entrepreneurs*. Oxford: Oxford University Press, 2022.

Pouteaux, Preston. *The Bees of Rainbow Falls: Finding Faith, Imagination and Delight in Your Neighbourhood*. Skyforest: Urban Loft, 2017.

– *The Neighbours Are Real and Other Beautiful Things: A Collection of Short Essays*. Chestermere: Plesion, 2020.

Putnam, Robert. *Bowling Alone: The Collapse and Revival of American Community*. New York: Simon & Schuster, 2001.

Rah, Soong-Chan. *Many Colors: Cultural Intelligence for a Changing Church, Prophetic Lament: A Call for Justice in Troubled Times*. Chicago: Moody, 2010.

– *The Next Evangelicalism: Freeing the Church from Western Cultural Captivity*. Downers Grove: IVP, 2009.

Rayside, David, Jerald Sabin, and Paul E.J. Thomas. *Religion and Canadian Party Politics*. Vancouver: UBC Press, 2017.

Reimer, Sam. *Caught in the Current: British and Canadian Evangelicals in an Age of Self-Spirituality*. Montreal & Kingston: McGill-Queen's University Press, 2023.

– *Evangelicals and the Continental Divide: The Conservative Protestant Subculture in Canada and the United States*. Montreal & Kingston: McGill-Queen's University Press, 2003.

Reimer, Sam, and Michael Wilkinson. *A Culture of Faith: Evangelical Congregations in Canada*. Montreal & Kingston: McGill-Queen's University Press, 2015.

Riphagen, Johannes. "Church-in-the-Neighbourhood: A Spatio-Theological Ethnography of Protestant Christian Place-Making in the Suburban Context of Lunetten." Unpublished PhD diss., 2021.

Rooms, Nigel, and Steve Taylor. *Ecclesial Futures*, Volume 1 (1). Eugene: Wipf & Stock, 2020.

– *Ecclesial Futures*, Volume 1 (2). Eugene: Wipf & Stock, 2020.

– *Ecclesial Futures*, Volume 2 (1). Eugene: Wipf & Stock, 2021.

Root, Andrew. *Churches and the Crisis of Decline: A Hopeful, Practical Ecclesiology for a Secular Age*. Grand Rapids: Baker Academic, 2022.

Roxburgh, Alan. *Introducing the Missional Church: What It Is, Why It Matters, How to Become One*. Grand Rapids: Baker, 2009.

– *Joining God, Remaking Church, Changing the World: The New Shape of the Church in Our Time*. New York: Morehouse, 2015.

– *Missional: Joining God in the Neighborhood*. Grand Rapids: Baker, 2011.

– *Missional Mapmaking: Skills for Leading in a Time of Transition*. San Francisco: Jossey-Bass, 2009.

– *Practices for the Refounding of God's People*. New York: Church Publishing, 2018.

– *Reaching a New Generation: Strategies for Tomorrow's Church*. Vancouver: Regent College Publishing, 1993.

– *Structured for Mission: Renewing the Culture of the Church*. Downers Grove: IVP, 2015.

Roxburgh, Alan, and Fred Romanuk. *The Missional Leader: Equipping Your Church to Reach a Changing World*. Minneapolis: Fortress, 2020.

Runyon, Dave, and Jay Pathak. *The Art of Neighboring: Building Genuine Relationships Right Outside Your Door*. Grand Rapids: Baker, 2012.

Sangaramoorthy, Thurka, and Karen Kroeger. *Rapid Ethnographic Assessments: A Practical Approach and Toolkit for Collaborative Community Research*. London: Routledge, 2020.

Santos, Narry, and Mark Naylor, eds. *Mission and Evangelism in a Secularizing World: Academy, Agency, and Assembly Perspectives from Canada*. Eugene: Pickwick, 2019.

Scharen, Christian. *Fieldwork in Theology: Exploring the Social Context of God's Work in the World*. Grand Rapids: Baker Academic, 2015.

Scharen, Christian, ed. *Explorations in Ecclesiology and Ethnography*. Grand Rapids: Eerdmans, 2012.

Scharen, Christian, and Aana Marie Vigen, eds. *Ethnography as Christian Theology and Ethics*. New York: Continuum, 2011.

Schuurman, Peter. *The Subversive Evangelical: The Ironic Charisma of an Irreligious Megachurch*. Montreal & Kingston: McGill-Queen's University Press, 2019.

Semple, Neil. *The Lord's Dominion: The History of Canadian Methodism*. Montreal & Kingston: McGill-Queen's University Press, 1996.

Sheldrake, Philip. *The Spiritual City: Theology, Spirituality and the Urban*. London: Wiley-Blackwell, 2014.

Shigematsu, Ken. *Survival Guide for the Soul*. Grand Rapids: Zondervan, 2018.

Silverman, David. *Interpreting Qualitative Data*. London: Sage, 2015.

Smith, Christian. *American Evangelicalism: Embattled and Thriving*. Chicago: University of Chicago Press, 1998.

– *Religion: What It Is, How It Works and Why It Matters*. Princeton: Princeton University Press, 2017.

Smith, Christian, and Patricia Snell. *Souls in Transition: The Religious and Spiritual Lives of Emerging Adults*. Oxford: Oxford University Press, 2009.

Smith, Gordon. *Wisdom from Babylon: Leadership for the Church in a Secular Age*. Downers Grove: IVP, 2020.

Smith, James K. *Desiring the Kingdom: Worship, Worldview and Cultural Formation*. Grand Rapids: Baker, 2009.

Smith, R. Drew, Stephanie C. Boddie, and Ronald E. Peters, eds. *Urban Ministry Reconsidered: Contexts and Approaches*. Louisville: Westminster/John Knox, 2018.

Stone, Bryan. *Finding Faith Today*. Eugene: Wipf & Stock, 2018.

Strhan, Anna. *Aliens and Strangers: The Struggle for Coherence in the Everyday Lives of Evangelicals*. Oxford: Oxford University Press, 2015.

Swinton, John, and Harriet Mowat. *Practical Theology and Qualitative Research*, 2nd ed., London: SCM, 2016.

Taylor, Charles. *Modern Social Imaginaries*. Duke: Duke University Press, 2004.

– *A Secular Age*. Cambridge: Belknap, 2007.

Thiessen, Joel. *The Meaning of Sunday: The Practice of Belief in a Secular Age*. Montreal & Kingston: McGill-Queen's University Press, 2015.

Thiessen, Joel, and Sarah Wilkins-LaFlamme. *None of the Above: Nonreligious Identity in the US and Canada*. Regina: University of Regina Press, 2020.

Todd, Douglas, ed. *Cascadia: The Elusive Utopia – Exploring the Spirit of the Northwest*. Vancouver: Ronsdale Press, 2008.

Toly, Noah J. *Cities of Tomorrow and the City to Come: A Theology of Urban Life*. Grand Rapids: Zondervan, 2015.

Van Gelder, Craig, and Dwight J. Zscheile, eds. *The Missional Church in Perspective: Mapping Trends and Shaping the Conversation*. Grand Rapids: Baker, 2011.

Walsh, H.H. *Volume One: A History of the Christian Church in Canada. The Church in the French Era*. Toronto: The Ryerson Press, 1966.

Ward, Pete. *Introducing Practical Theology: Mission, Ministry and the Life of the Church*. Grand Rapids: Baker, 2017.

– *Liquid Church*. Eugene: Wipf & Stock, 2002.

Ward, Pete, ed. *Perspectives on Ecclesiology and Ethnography*. Grand Rapids: Eerdmans, 2012.

Ward, Pete, and Knut Tveitereid, eds. *The Wiley Blackwell Companion to Theology and Qualitative Research*. Hoboken: Wiley Blackwell, 2022.

Watkins, Clare. *Disclosing Church: An Ecclesiology Learned from Conversations in Practice*. London: Routledge, 2020.

White, Aaron. *Recovering: From Brokenness and Addiction to Blessedness and Community*. Grand Rapids: Baker, 2020.

White, Vera, and Charles Wiley. *New Worshipping Communities: A Theological Exploration*. Louisville: Westminster/John Knox, 2018.

Wigg-Stevenson, Natalie. *Ethnographic Theology: An Inquiry into the Production of Theological Knowledge*. New York: Palgrave MacMillan, 2014.

Wilkins-Laflamme, Sarah. *Religion, Spirituality and Secularity among Millennials: The Generation Shaping American and Canadian Trends*. London: Routledge, 2023.

Williams, Paul. *Exiles on Mission: How Christians Can Thrive in a Post-Christian World*. Grand Rapids: Brazos, 2020.

Wilson, Jonathan. *God's Good World: Reclaiming the Doctrine of Creation*. Grand Rapids: Eerdmans, 2013.

Wilson-Raybould, Jody. *From Where I Stand: Rebuilding Indigenous Nations for a Stronger Canada*. Vancouver: Purich Books/UBC Press, 2019.

Wirzba, Norman. *From Nature to Creation: A Christian Vision for Understanding and Loving Our World*. Grand Rapids: Baker Academic, 2015.

Wolterstorff, Nicholas. *Art in Action*. Carlisle: Paternoster, 1997.

Woodley, Randy. *Indigenous Theology and the Western Worldview: A Decolonized Approach to Christian Doctrine*. Grand Rapids: Baker, 2022.

Yee, Paul. *Saltwater City: A History of the Chinese in Vancouver*. Vancouver: Douglas & McIntyre, 2006.

Yong, Amos. *The Spirit Poured Out on All Flesh: Pentecostalism and the Possibility of Global Theology*. Grand Rapids: Baker, 2005.

Zuckerman, Phil, and John Shook. *The Oxford Handbook of Secularism*. Oxford: Oxford University Press, 2017.

Index

p47 want to change the topic